WHERE SOCIALISM FAILED
An Actual Experiment

By STEWART GRAHAME

Updated
With new illustrations, Appendices,
And notes
Photographs courtesy of The University of Sydney

First Published by
JOHN MURRAY, ALBEMARLE STREET, LONDON
1912

Contents

" Socialists have this advantage over their opponents, that, while it is very easy to inveigh against the evils of society as we know it, it is very difficult to prove the imperfection of Utopias which have never been brought to the test of experience. Mr. Grahame's description of a concrete instance is therefore a valuable addition to the controversy. Socialism is sometimes represented as the inevitable result of the sufferings of mankind, and Marx and others have sought to give scientific precision to this idea. Australian Socialism, however, came as a bolt from the blue; it arose among a population comparatively prosperous. The driving force of the Socialist agitation comes, we believe, neither from science nor from suffering, but from a form of religious fanaticism which appeals to its devotees as a call to a holy war."

- The Spectator, April 23rd, 1910.

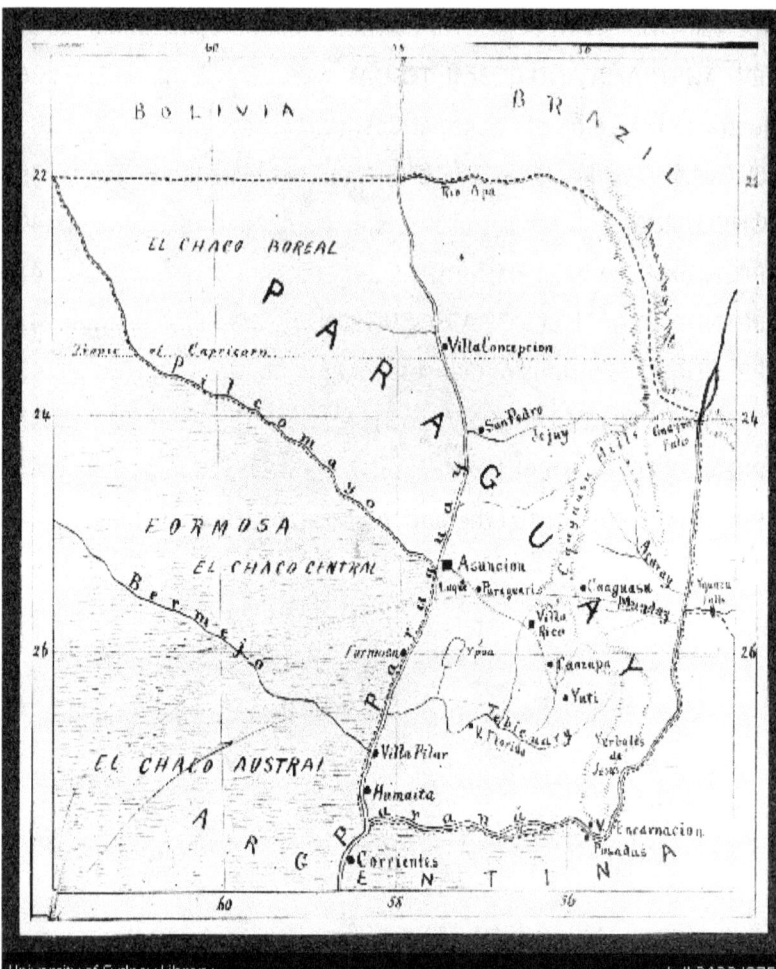

INTRODUCTION.

In his introduction to 'The Socialist Movement,' Mr. Ramsay Macdonald, M.P., complains that "One of the greatest of the difficulties which beset the path of the Socialist is the refusal on the part of his opponents to give an accurate statement of what Socialism means and what the purpose of Socialism is."

It would appear therefore that a clear statement of what Socialism meant, and how it worked, in a particular instance where it was tried in practice, should be of value to Socialist seekers after truth as well as to the general public. 'Where Socialism Failed' is a straightforward account of William Lane's bold attempt to realise 'Socialism in our Time' at New Australia and Cosme in Paraguay.

Although most of the matter in the present work is fresh, about one-fifth of the text has appeared before in the 'Conservative and Unionist' (published by The National Conservative Union), or in the pamphlets "New Australia" (published by H. E. Morgan), and 'Socialism: An Actual Experiment' (published by the Anti-Socialist Union).

It was in consequence of the welcome accorded to 'New Australia' in the Press and in the constituencies, and the many requests for fuller information, made by Socialists in particular, that the present work was undertaken. I take this opportunity of assuring Socialist friends that the book is not a mere compilation. I am no stranger in old Australia, and have slept over five hundred nights in a mud hut at 'New Australia'. My own information concerning every detail of life at William Lane's two settlements was obtained, by word of mouth, direct from leading figures in the Association, from documents supplied by them, and from personal observation and experience. Extensive use has been made of quotations from articles, letters, etc., by those in sympathy with the movement, and of official reports, principally as a means of setting independent confirmatory evidence before the reader.

Stewart Grahame
Authors' Club,
April, 1912.

CHAPTER I.

THE GREAT STRIKE.

The Australian Socialist party commenced its career as an active fighting force in 1889, the first manifestation of its might falling like a bombshell, not at home, but in Great Britain. When the London dock labourers came out on strike — an unorganised mob not affiliated to any great and wealthy trade union — it was freely prophesied that sheer starvation would drive them back to work within a short time. The prophets were disappointed, however, for, to the surprise of most people in England, including the strikers themselves, their meager funds were reinforced by a contribution of £30,000 cabled from Brisbane, and thus assisted, the dock labourers gained the day.

Considering the fact that Australia is so sparsely inhabited it was considered a remarkable thing that so large a sum could be raised from a section of its workers, almost in a moment for the purpose of taking sides in a dispute with which they had no concern, for the benefit of men they had never met.

In fact, the incident pointed not merely to the existence of a wealthy Labour organisation in the Antipodes but also to a new spirit of unselfishness in Trade Unionism, which suggested some very exceptional influence in the background.

Those who troubled to probe into the matter further discovered that the central figure of the Australian Socialist movement was a journalist named William Lane, an individual who figures so prominently in the following narrative that it will be as well to visualise him without delay, as seen by his own supporters.

"Born into English agricultural life, with Irish and Cornish blood in his veins, with an adventurous spirit, inherited from the old seafaring stock from which he sprang," one of his warmest admirers says of him, "the dreamy, studious boy, 'armed from birth, learned early to ponder on the sufferings of the labouring class to which he belonged. The hard struggle and premature age of his mother in particular, sank into his heart, inspiring a chivalrous respect for women in the abstract, and a practical sympathy for the working-woman in the concrete, which characterises him to this day. When not thirsting for a sea-life, picking up scraps of Latin from a somewhat superior, village school-master, or busy with the many tasks allotted to the children of the poor, the boy Lane was studying problems with large, short-sighted blue eyes, and learning to clothe his thoughts in language culled from the Bible and the Pilgrim's Progress. At the age of fifteen we find him in America, earning his own bread, learning the compositors' work, picking up Yankee cuteness with the Yankee twang, devoting all his spare time to reading, and preserving the nerve and bravado which enabled him defiantly to swim a rapid shunned by his companions as fatal. It is this indomitable 'pluck', in an apparently frail body, which has stood him in good stead in later days, enabling him to surmount obstacles before which many a stout-hearted man would have quailed. From the compositors' he drifted into the reporters' room, and was soon wielding a vigorous pen. Some few years later, having married a large-hearted, broad-minded wife, American-bred, but grand-daughter of a shrewd Scottish University professor, William Lane migrated to Queensland, and became one of the most successful free-lances on the Australian press."

At first Lane worked on the Observer and devoted his burning pen entirely to the cause of suffering humanity. Wherever there was an overcrowded slum or a case of sweated labour, William

Lane would ferret it out and hold up to public scorn those who were responsible for such evil conditions There probably never lived a more single-minded man, and his honesty of purpose was so clearly recognised that he won the confidence of the working classes completely.

It was Lane's fervent desire "to idealise Labour, to conquer want, and hate, and greed, and vice, and establish peace on earth and good-will towards men."

Thousands of other thinkers have desired to see the same beautiful programme realised, though most have despaired of its possibility on this planet. With his optimistic temperament, however, William Lane was convinced that there really did exist, ready to hand, a simple remedy for all the ills that mar the civilised world. It was his firm conviction that, if capitalism and the wages system were utterly abolished and a State established in accordance with Socialistic theories, envy, hatred, malice and all uncharitableness would utterly disappear from the earth; crime would be no more, human nature would be automatically purged of all its unlovely features, heaven on earth would be a fact for every man, woman and child.

Since he held such beliefs it was not wonderful that Lane strained every nerve to obtain converts. He rapidly gained an extraordinary ascendancy over the minds of the intelligent artisans and mechanics of Brisbane, and disseminated among them, by means of tracts, free reading rooms and Socialistic debating societies, the fascinating fictions of Bellamy and the startling doctrines of Karl Marx and his disciples. His weekly paper, The Boomerang, met with instant success, and served as a medium for reaching the miners and shearers in the back-blocks, who fell under the spell of his glamorous phrases as readily as the townsfolk had done. This much accomplished, he tackled the leaders of the various great Trade Unions and converted them to his theory that it would be possible, by concerted action, to overthrow capital and confiscate land and all means of production for the exclusive benefit of the manual worker. Then he proved his own adhesion to the new creed by leaving his highly remunerative position, and moving into a common workman's cottage, prior to establishing a new journal on co-operative lines. This new journal, which scored an instant success, was entitled The Worker, and had for its war-cry the motto 'Socialism in our Time.' In it he ran as a serial Bellamy's convert-making story 'Looking Backward.' His aims are well summed up in Mr. Blatchford's statement:

"Practical Socialism is so simple that a child may understand it. It is a kind of national scheme of co-operation managed by the State. Its programme consists essentially of one demand, that the land and other instruments of production shall be the common property of the people, and shall be used and governed by the people for the people."

With his magnetic personality Lane seemed like a heaven-sent prophet to the eager band of disciples who gathered about him and devoted all their energies to disseminating his doctrines. Of a truth there was something very attractive about them to the wage-earners, for it was Lane's amazing creed, that the factory-hand was the rightful owner of the factory, that the sheep-shearer was entitled to the full profits of the shearing industry, that the legal owners of all forms of property were robbing the manual workers of their dues. Among his followers the fallacious theory that "the frugal workman only gets about one-third of his earnings, while under Socialism he, the worker, would get all his earnings," found ready acceptance.

Wherever manual workers were gathered together, the vividly written columns of The Worker were scanned, and its burning phrases discussed with eager interest. It was thus that William Lane became a power in the land, a man who was literally worshipped by thousands; who had only to bemoan the miseries of certain strikers in another land to open the purse strings of all who followed him on their behalf. It was not mere philanthropy, but a far deeper-seated motive which moved William Lane to take the action he did with regard to the London dockers. He wanted to give the world a powerful demonstration of what could be accomplished, if only 'the workers' would broaden their outlook and fight each other's battles as well as their own. The principle is a well-recognised one now, but it was novel then.

"William Lane dreamed of a federated unionism which should link together all the component parts of the labour world," explains Mr. Rose-Soley. "It was with this object that he mixed himself up with strikes, albeit recognising, with most far-seeing thinkers, the absolute futility of strikes save as an evidence of strength and solidarity; it was with this object that he cemented the bonds between labour in far-apart lands, instigating the magnificent contribution of the Brisbane wharf labourer to his starving brother, the London docker."

It so happened that Australia at that time was tottering on the verge of a financial crisis. For ten years the 'Working Man's Paradise' had lived on credit. Now the time of reckoning was at hand, and only a succession of prosperous years, unhampered by labour troubles, could pull things through. It was an anxious time for all, and for the pastoralists in particular. Would the shearers, who had shared in their good times, stand by them during the crisis? Would 'labour' combine for its own sake and that of the country, to save Australia from bankruptcy? A thousand times, no! The Trade Unions coffers were full, and here was the heaven-sent chance to smash 'capital' in the

Antipodes. The formidable A.L.F. (Australian Labour Federation) which the great Unions had set up, seized the opportunity to issue a manifesto calling upon the State to nationalise all forms of property and to institute the just division amongst all citizens of the State of all wealth production, less only that part retained for public and common requirements.

What the Paris Commune had failed to effect in France they hoped to achieve at one blow in Australia, which was to become a Paradise of Socialism. By first smashing the pastoralists, and then turning the battering ram of their organisation against each smaller interest in turn they expected to triumph. It was the declared object of the Federation to attack the competitive system and openly commence a campaign which will not cease until Capitalism — that is the private holding by a few of the means whereby all must live - is no more.

An excuse for the opening of a conflict was found in a dispute between certain shearers and the pastoralists, which led to the engagement by the latter of a number of non-unionist shearers to take the place of those on strike. At once the Shearers' Union took up the position — since grown only too familiar to English employers of labour — of refusing to work where non-unionists were also employed.

Furthermore the Wharf Labourers' Union intimated that they would handle no wool shorn by 'black-legs', and declared a sympathetic strike. Next, the merchant marine were induced to join the movement, and both officers and men left their ships. Then the coal-miners of Newcastle (N.S.W.) refused to hew coal intended for the ships whose crews were on strike, and the colliery owners locked them out.

When the General Strike was in full swing all trades and industries were paralysed throughout Queensland, New South Wales, Victoria and New Zealand from August till October, 1890, even the over-seas shipping lay idle in the harbours, and the strikers neglected no means to make their boycott of all forms of work effective. Non-unionists engaged in carting wool through the streets were charged by the strikers whose Union officials could no longer control them, and the trolleys flung into the sea. The Queensland strikers formed huge camps in the bush and incendiarism was frequent. The principal towns were in a state of siege, and, on the 19th September, a pitched battle was fought between police and mounted troops on the one hand, and the determined mobs on the other.

Towards the end of the year some sort of truce was patched up, but in 1891 the trouble broke out again, and once more in 1892. In the latter year a special train taking non-unionist labour from Adelaide to replace strikers at the Broken Hill silver mines, was attacked by an armed mob, who not only stoned but also fired bullets at the strike-breakers. On a number of the ringleaders being imprisoned, howling rioters stormed the gaol determined to tear it down, just as the Parisians levelled the Bastille. In fact, red revolution raged in the Antipodes for nearly two years before it spent its strength and the A.L.F. sulkily admitted defeat, and allowed its members to return to work in the ordinary manner.

How the Trade Union leaders must have cursed the day they projected the General Strike, when they counted the cost of that two years' wicked, wasteful strife! To say nothing of the many millions of pounds lost to trade in Australia (about which the Federation did not concern itself) the strikers had lost £2,000,000 in wages, the Trade Union coffers were emptied, the leaders' credit gone, their power broken. Partly as a result of the disastrous strikes the long-threatened financial catastrophe descended upon Australia in 1892-3 and banks with liabilities of £134,000,000 suspended payment.

The A.L.F had demonstrated its strength, truly, but only as blind Samson proved his, when he broke the pillars which supported the roof in the house of the Philistines, and was himself crushed in the ruin which descended upon his enemies.

Note : — When the straggle broke out once more in 1894, it was conducted with even greater acrimony. The following memorandum, by an eye-witness, conveys an idea of how the unscrupulous will take advantage of a purely trade dispute to promote the 'class war.'
"It became evident that there was a large body who were not merely bent on compelling the employers to alter the agreement, but who rather regarded the whole struggle as an episode in the great struggle between labour and capital," remarks Mr. O. M. L. Lester in the Economic Review. "These men carried on a real and bitter warfare against capital in every shape and form. Not only did they brutally bully and ill-treat 'black-legs' but they succeeded also in destroying the woolsheds at Ayrshire Downs, Cassilis, Bedcliffe, Cambridge Downs, Earongella, Mannca, and Oondooroo, and Dagworth. The shooting case at Coombe Martin and the night attack on Dagworth are further evidences of the bitterness of this particular party. I do not believe that the actions of these violent persons met with the approval of the better sort of unionists, but it is significant that no Labour member to my knowledge, nor any Labour paper as far as I am aware, expressed any sense of shame at the excesses of their advanced guard. Moreover, pamphlets of the inflammatory kind common to the revolutionary and the penny novelist, were widely circulated throughout the colony, urging men to useless crime.

In one of these wonderful productions Parliaments are described as 'committees of corpulent robbers and polished thieves, oratorical prostitutes and abject hirelings.'

"The Tree of Liberty only bears fruit when manured with the bones of the fat usurers and insolent despots." Another of the same kind urges men to "study the science of death, use bullets, steel, melinite, kerosene, lithofracteur poison, blasting powder." Finally, it says, "You must steal like Spartans, think like heroes, lie like hell."

CHAPTER II.

A BETTER NAPOLEON.

As there has been a good deal of misapprehension on this subject, it should be clearly understood that the Labour Federation's attack on Capital was simply an act of aggression, with Syndicalism as its object. The battle was not fought by the Unions on legitimate grounds in defence of some overworked or underpaid members. Employers of Labour were under the thumb of the Unions, whose yoke was grievous to bear, and wages ruled higher, with shorter hours, than in any other country of the world.

In 1883 navvies and general labourers received a minimum of 8s. daily, blacksmiths los., painters and carpenters 11s, stonemasons 11s, plasterers 13s., and bricklayers 12s. 6d. Four years later wages fell somewhat, though they were still very high, in 1888 they bounded up again, and rose once more in 1889. Thus on the eve of the Great Strike Australia might truly be called the 'Working Man's Paradise.' Now, observe how Trade Union greed, like the monkey with the nuts in a familiar fable, defeated its own object, and, by seeking to grasp all, lost most of what it had already secured. In bringing about the ruin of the Capitalist, the Labour Federation was startled to discover that it had also ruined 'Labour.' By the end of 1895, wages had fallen below the level at which they stood before the commencement of Trade Union activity in 1850.

Thus the great plot recoiled upon the heads of the Trade Unions and its promoters admitted their mistake. But when the Trade Union officials were in the depths of despair over the proved inefficiency of strike methods, the way to snatch a victory from defeat was pointed out by William Lane and his chosen band of associates — men who in the strange condition of Australia at that time, might be barristers, university graduates, ex-bank managers, or highly trained journalists although they happened to be earning their livelihood as shearers, storekeepers or miners.

"Since Labour alone produces wealth," they argued, "it is still possible to checkmate Capital by withdrawing Labour, not temporarily by means of another strike, but bodily to a new country, where none but the workers themselves shall profit by their industry."

Foreseeing that the slump in wages would give a great impetus to such a movement. Lane began in 1890 to project a plan so daring, and so unprecedented, that at first few people believed that it could be seriously contemplated. However, on this occasion, as always, Lane was in grim earnest, and issued his ultimatum to Capital in the form of the following Declaration of Principles:

Whereas -
So long as one depends upon another for leave to work and so long as the selfishness induced by the uncertainty of living prevents mankind from seeing that it is best for all to insure one another against all possibility of social degradation, true Liberty and Happiness are impossible ; and
Whereas -
The weakness, ignorance, and doubts of society at large is the great barrier in the way of the establishment of such true social order as will insure to every citizen security against want and opportunity to develop to the fullest the faculties evolving in Humanity;
Therefore —

It is desirable and imperative that by a community wherein all labour in common for the common good actual proof shall be given that under conditions which render it impossible for one to tyrannize over another, and which declare the first duty of each to be the well-being of all and the sole duty of all to be the well-being of each, men and women can live in comfort, happiness, intelligence and orderliness unknown in a society where none can be sure today that they or their children will not starve tomorrow.

With this end in view an Association of Workers is hereby instituted, . . . the signatories intending and expecting to migrate to another country there to devote to the movement their possessions and their best endeavours.

It was at first supposed by most thinking people in Australia that William Lane would find few to back his remarkable project, but circumstances were in his favour. The Queensland Bush was still full of strikers' camps, where hundreds of capable and able-bodied shearers found themselves stranded and unable to obtain work, because many pastoralists were ruined and others were employing non-unionists only.

Unlike the shearers of a by-gone day, who were notoriously illiterate, stupid and drunken the average modern shearer is sober, shrewd, and hardheaded, and perhaps the most argumentative man on earth. As a rule he has great notions on the subject of equality, and a considerable portion of his ample leisure is spent in reading and re-reading the interesting writings of Messrs. Bellamy, Blatchford, Karl Marx and Belfort Bax, and arguing with his mates upon them. He religiously takes in some weekly paper devoted to a red-hot Socialist propaganda, and believes himself exceptionally well-informed upon the course of all affairs that matter throughout the universe. Among such men as these, already so far converted to his way of thinking that they held as a simple statement of fact the saying that all save manual workers are thieves and parasites upon the rest of the community; Lane was confident of finding fruit ripe for his plucking.

In the remote Bush, moreover, there were thousands of others not concerned in — who might not even have heard of — the Great Strike. There were, for instance, the 'free selectors' in the backblocks, living wretchedly upon the land from which the once wealthy squatters had been driven, where they had been dumped and forgotten by a Socialistic Government. In equally bad case were the small capitalists, whose farms or orchards had gone to ruin because the artificially maintained cost of labour made hired help impossible. As a newspaper put it: "the country is languishing for the labour congested in the Metropolis. Private enterprise is dying, being slowly killed by Government competition. Dairymen are turning their farms into sheep-runs because they cannot get Labour; fruit in the orchards is rotting on the trees or on the ground from the same cause. The selectors in Gippsland especially are crippled; they find it impossible to get their land cleared. But everywhere through the State there is the same complaint of scarcity of Labour . . . the Government has raised the rate of wages to seven shillings a day; the labourer naturally prefers the Government stroke and can be tempted away from that easy and pleasant way of passing his time only by an increased rate of wages. That increased rate very few industries can afford to pay ; thus all enterprise is crushed."

Having an intimate acquaintance with their troubles Lane foresaw that a sufficient bait would catch the selectors and small capitalists by hundreds ; but the bait must be sufficient. To tempt them to join his scheme he recognised that the appeal must be a personal one. and that the missionary of his movement must possess the enthusiasm and personal magnetism of an inspired prophet.

"Is not the only hope in the rising of a better Napoleon?" he demanded. "In the elevation of a leader with the brain of a Jay Gould and the heart of a Christ?"

After careful consideration William Lane decided to undertake the work himself. Turning over the editorship of The Worker to other hands, he set forth upon his whirlwind mission, sustained by a perfect faith in the righteousness of his cause — for Lane believed every word of what he preached. To him "Looking Backward" was no delightfully ingenious fiction ; he was convinced that the counterpart of everything described in Bellamy's book might be set up in real life. It was this absolute belief in the beneficence of his mission which gave Lane his convincing power. When he dismounted from his horse at sundown at some isolated shearing-shed — caked with dust and stiff from long riding, his throat parched and his head aching from the sun — weariness slipped from him as if by magic when the shearers gathered about him and he broached the one theme which he had ridden so far to open to them. Or, in the lonely Bush, he would halt by some camp-fire and puff his pipe in company with the other wayfarers gathered round its genial flare. At first the conversation would be upon indifferent subjects, maybe, but when they realized that their visitor was 'John Miller' (as he signed himself of The Worker, an expectant hush would fall upon the little assembly, and Lane needed no urging to talk for hour on hour about the glories of the Promised Land, to which he would lead them if they would only trust him.

What an asset such a man would have been as the organiser of some saner plan of social amelioration! And yet, who knows? it may be that the warning provided by the failure of this earnest, but mistaken enthusiast, will be of more service to the present and future generations than his moderate success in some less ambitious direction, would have been.

Mere lip-service, or formal assent to the doctrines he taught, would not satisfy Lane. When once he discovered that he had won a man's secret sympathies, he did not rest until that man was converted to the necessity for action.

"All that any religion has been to the highest thought of any people, Socialism is, and more, to those who conceive it aright," he declared, "without blinding us to our own weaknesses and wickedness, without offering to us any sophistry, or cajoling us with any fallacy, it enthrones Love above the universe, gives us hope for all who are downtrodden, and restores to us faith in the eternal fitness of things. Socialism is indeed a religion — demanding deeds as well as words. Not until professing Socialists understand this will the world at large see Socialism as it really is."

As it happened, William Lane was not alone just then in projecting a scheme for the establishment of a perfect State where all should be free and equal.

Early in 1890 Herr Theodor Hertzka (at one time economic editor to the Neue Freie Presse) published in Vienna his 'Freeland — A Social Anticipation'[i] of which Interesting work an English translation appeared in 1891. Being written by an acknowledged authority on economic questions, this closely-reasoned Utopian romance attracted a great deal of attention, and a 'Freeland Association' was formed on the Continent for the purpose of putting its teachings into practice. With apparently flaw-less logic, Herr Hertzka proved that in a state so ideally, yet simply, organised as Freeland, such universal luxury would be enjoyed that it would seem 'as if each Freelander without exception had about 120 slaves at his disposal.'[ii] "What wonder that we can live like masters," one of his characters remarks, "notwithstanding that servitude is un-known in Freeland." In addition, within twenty-five years of its foundation, the joint-wealth equally enjoyed by the 26,000,000 inhabitants of Freeland, amounts "without taking into account the incalculable value of the soil — to £1300 per head, or £6000 per family."

Of course the English edition of this work found its way to Australia, and prepared a harvest ready to be reaped by William Lane. Probably also it greatly encouraged him to go forward with his proposal, although on somewhat different lines. But then the readers of 'Freeland' were prepared for some slight variations in the scheme, for, in his preface (see Appendix F), Hertzka himself said, "I do not imagine that the establishment of the future social order must necessarily be effected exactly in the way described in the following pages... If economic freedom and justice are to obtain in human society, they must be seriously determined upon; and it seems easier to unite a few thousands in such a determination than numberless millions, most of whom are not accustomed to accept the new — let it be ever so clear and self-evident — until it has been embodied in fact."

That was precisely the view which William Lane was so fond of urging. He planned to commence his ideal State with not more than about 800 families. When they had embodied in fact, for the whole world to see, the wonderful prosperity and happiness to be enjoyed under Socialism, he believed that all civilised peoples would hasten to embrace its benefits also.

The name which Lane decided to give his Socialist paradise was 'New Australia' but this did not imply that only Australians were welcomed; people of any nationality might join, provided they were not coloured. It was his design to send propagandist missionaries to Great Britain, South Africa and Canada as soon as a suitable territory had been found and a nucleus settlement established. Simultaneously with his own recruiting campaign, he sent forth three trusted emissaries, Walker, Leek and Saunders, all experienced bushmen, to prospect a site for his new Canaan. His instructions to them were identical in character with those which Moses gave to Joshua and his companions:

"See the land what it is; and the people that dwelleth therein, whether they be strong or weak, few or many;
And what the land is that they dwell in, whether it be good or bad; and what cities they be that they dwell in, whether in tents, or in strongholds; And what the land is, whether it be fat or lean, whether there be wood therein, or not" - Numbers xiii. 18-20.

But Lane's plan of procedure differed in this vital respect from that of Moses; that whereas the latter relied wholly upon God to give his followers secure possession of 'a land which floweth with milk and honey,' it was a basic principle with William Lane to exclude the Deity from any participation in the affairs of New Australia. As will be seen from the official 'Basis' below, it was laid down that religion would not be recognised by Lane's community.

The following is the exact text of the Constitution, which all who joined the New Australia Co-operative Settlement Association signed, and pledged themselves loyally to observe.

BASIS OF CO-OPERATIVE ORGANISATION,

Production. Ownership by the community of all the means of production in exchange and distribution. Conduct by the community of all production in exchange and distribution.

At a later date the Constitution was altered in certain important respects. (See Appendix C).

BASIS OF ORGANISATION
Superintendence by the community of all labour-saving co-operations.
Allotment. Maintenance by the community of children under guardianship of parents.
Maintenance by the community of all sanitary and educational establishments.
Saving by the community of all capital needed by the community.
Division of remaining wealth production among all adult members of the community equally, without regard to sex, age, office, or physical or mental capacity.
Authority. Subject to the supremacy of the laws of the state settled in, which all members pledge themselves to observe loyally, the following authority and regulations shall be observed between the members of the community.
Ballot vote of all adult members to be supreme authority.
Director, elected by two-thirds majority of general ballot, to be sole executive authority, advised by Board of Superintendents.

Superintendents, elected by two-thirds majority of departmental ballot, to be sole departmental authorities^ subject to director.
Regulations. Regulations affecting the community at large to be confirmed by a two-thirds majority of all adult members.
Departmental regulations to be confirmed by a majority

of all adult members interested.

All regulations to be submitted annually for continuation or rejection.

Disputes arising between the community and any member or members to be decided in equity by an arbitrator mutually agreed upon between the communal authority and the member or members interested.

Disputes arising between members to be decided in equity by an arbitrator mutually agreed upon by them.

Dismissal from the community, for persistent or unpardonable offence against the well-being of the community, to be decreed only by a five-sixth majority of all adult members.

Elections. All offices to be vacated annually and whenever occupants cease to retain the confidence of their constituents.

Individuality. The individuality of every member in thought, religion, speech and leisure, and in all matters whatsoever whereby the individuality of others is not affected to be held inviolable.

Sex Equality. The sexes to be recognised as equally entitled to full membership.

Religion. Religion not to be officially recognised by the community.

Amendment. Amendment of this basis for co-operative organisation to be made only by a two-thirds majority of all adult members.

FINANCIAL CLAUSES,

Agreement. Every member of the association, by act of joining the association, agrees to subscribe to the funds of the association all he may possess when he is finally enrolled for actual migration, such subscription to be not less than £60.

Preliminary Expenses. The necessary funds for all preliminary expenses, including prospecting organisation, and colonisation arrangements, shall be provided by a preliminary payment of

£10, £s of which must be paid within one month of provisional enrolment, the other £s within three months of provisional enrolment : this £10 to be counted as part of the £60 which is fixed as the minimum final subscription. Return of Payments. The payment of £10 for preliminary expenses and the final subscription of not less than an additional £5 shall both be, when made, free and voluntary donations to the board of trustees for the purposes of the association which no member shall reclaim if he decides, after having made either, to with-draw from membership. But any member shall be entitled to reclaim any amount over £10 which he may have paid to the board of trustees in advance for and on account of his final subscription should he decide, before final enrolment for migration, to withdraw from membership. The board of trustees, if for any reason whatever it decides to strike from the roll any member who has fulfilled to the time of such striking off all the conditions of membership, shall return him his previous payments in full.

Widowed Mothers. A subscription of ;£30 will be required for widowed mothers accompanying sons to the settlement. Exceptions at discretion of trustees.

Men over Fifty. At the discretion of the trustees a minimum subscription of ;£100 may be required of men over 50 years of age applying for membership.

Estimated Final, Contribution. Every member on joining shall state the estimated amount of his intended final contribution, and the delegate enrolling shall certify that such is a fair estimate to the best of his knowledge and belief.

Premium for Children Every family enrolled after June 12, 1893, to be charged a premium of £10 for every child over one year of age, this premium to be added to the final payment of not less than £5. Exceptions at discretion of trustees.

The Liquor Question. Without prejudice to the liquor question members shall pledge themselves to teetotalism until the initial difficulties of settlement have passed, and the Constitution been established.

With the circulars giving these particulars of the New Australia movement, the following notification was issued:
"This Association, organized upon the above lines, is in full accord with the Organisation of Labour, and has been recognized as such by all the great bush unions of Australia and by the Queensland A.L.F. General Council. Nearly half a million acres have been selected by its own prospectors in Paraguay and conceded it by the Government of that country. This land will never be sold but used to build up co-operative settlement. There is no humbug about New Australia."

CHAPTER III.

THE PROMISED LAND.

In selecting a site for New Australia Lane was guided by the following principles laid down by Hertzka for his 'Freeland' experiment:
"In carrying out our programme a hitherto unappropriated large tract of land will have to be acquired for the founding of an independent community. The question now is, what part of the earth shall we choose for such a purpose? For obvious reasons we cannot look for territory to any part of Europe; and everywhere in Asia, at least in those parts in which Caucasian races could flourish, we should be continually coming into collision with ancient forms of law and society. We might expect that the several governments in America and Australia would readily grant us land and freedom of action; but even there our young community would scarcely be able to enjoy that undisturbed quiet and security against antagonistic interference which would be at first a necessary condition of rapid and uninterrupted success."

The learned doctor came to the conclusion that such a tract of ground as he desired could be found only in Africa; William Lane, however, turned his attention to South America with its equally great natural resources still awaiting development. From his point of view there were strong arguments in favour of Paraguay as a suitable place for a large body of energetic Anglo-Saxons to settle in, since that State was one of the most prosperous of the Latin republics until the disastrous war of 1865-70 brought it to utter ruin. To restore the country to its old prosperity nothing more was (or is at the present day) needed than the introduction of a great many suitable immigrants, not afraid of work and capable of hard pioneering labour.

In the middle of the nineteenth century Paraguay was the most progressive State in South America, with so many flourishing industries that it was quite self-contained and economically independent of the rest of the world. It was the first country in South America to be provided with a railway.

"When Solano Lopez succeeded to the headship of the State in 1862 it possessed a respectable standing army and a large trained reserve, a squadron of gun-boats capable of meeting anything that floated on River Plate waters; a series of fortified places on the eastern bank of the Paraguay; an arsenal, a gun foundry and a large sum of money in the national coffers," the Paraguayan Consul once proudly stated before the Society of Arts, "but alas the mad ambitions of an autocrat brought irretrievable ruin upon the country. In the short period of eight years the vast resources of which Marshal Lopez came into possession had completely disappeared. The soldiers were lying dead upon the field of battle, the national treasury was empty, the flotilla had been captured, the arsenal and forts had been turned into heaps of ruins, the happy and prosperous land had been devastated, the towns and villages destroyed, the rich pasture lands denuded of their cattle, the population reduced from upwards of a million to one quarter of that number and that remnant composed of women and children; not a man was left to till the ground, not an ox to draw the plough, and Lopez himself, the origin of all this misery and ruin, had died sword in hand upon the banks of the Aquidaban."

During that terrible war against the combined armies of Brazil, the Argentine, and Uruguay, not only did the practice of all industries die out but every skilled worker perished, so that the

Paraguayans of the next generation grew up ignorant of the arts in which their forbears were skilled and, for the most part, reverted to a primitive way of living not far removed from savagery. Moreover the owners of hundreds of square miles of land had perished, without leaving a single member of their families to succeed them ; even the title deeds had vanished and for many rich estates the Government could find no claimants. Thus it came about that almost the whole area of the Republic was 'nationalised' as completely as the most ardent Socialist could wish, and vast tracts of country of untold richness became available, and were freely offered, for settlement, to those who could help to re-establish the industries and develop the great natural resources of the country.

In spite of its many advantages Lane's three prospectors did not immediately visit Paraguay, since the Argentine government was equally anxious to secure good immigrants, and offered large tracts of land on tempting settlement conditions. But the Australians had orders not to conclude a bargain until they were fully satisfied as to (1) climate, (2) soil, (3) water, (4) timber, and (5) ease of access, together with the friendly disposition of the Government and the security of life and property, and so were not easy to please. For many months they scoured the country and admitted that much of it was admirable for sheep raising, but the more accessible parts of the Argentine were long since taken up and had reached inflated values; anything within reach of their means, or offered practically for nothing, was in the far south or in the remote wilderness towards the Andes. At the Welsh colony at Chubut, to which they had been referred as an example of what courageous pioneers could accomplish, the prospectors heard dismal tales of ruined harvests, in successive seasons, due to floods, and frost. Elsewhere they were told of droughts almost as severe as those from which Australia suffers; in other parts they were disheartened by the flat uninteresting look of the untimbered country, to say nothing of the difficulty of communication. Moreover, while the Government was most anxious to attract some thousands of able-bodied immigrants, it was scarcely prepared to concede such a measure of autonomy as they demanded. Finally, after months of fruitless negotiations and much weary riding, the prospectors decided to leave the Argentine, at least for a time, and inspect Paraguay.

Undeterred by the reckless misstatements which the people of the River Plate ports jealously circulated concerning the bloodthirstiness of the amiable Paraguayans, Saunders and Leek boarded a river steamer and visited Asuncion. President Gonzales and Dr. Lopez, the Foreign Minister, welcomed them cordially and at once won their hearts by agreeing to let them establish an 'imperium in imperio' secure against interference from any provincial officials and subject only to the supreme Government. Contrary to what they had been led to believe in Buenos Aires, they found the Paraguayans, and particularly the graceful women, possessed of a sunnier temperament and far more winning manners than the rather staid Argentines.

The resident Englishmen, of whom there were quite a number, assured them that life and property were, if anything, safer in Paraguay than in the Argentine, moreover they discovered that land of equally good quality could be purchased for less than one-tenth of what it would cost in the latter country.

As he journeyed with them towards the territory which he considered would be ideal for the New Australia settlement, Senor Lopez informed the prospectors that they were by no means the first to dream of establishing a Socialist Paradise in Paraguay. Indeed his country owed the comparative civilisation of its Guarani inhabitants to the fact that they were rescued from savagery at the beginning of the seventeenth century by the founders of the 'Christian Republic,' under which 100,000 persons lived a Communistic life for 150 years. He quoted the testimony of many writers, themselves inimical to the Jesuits, to prove that the citizens of their thirty Communistic towns enjoyed a prosperity and happiness comparable with that of the inhabitants of Bacon's 'New Atlantis.' Even Voltaire, that arch-enemy of the Jesuits, described their establishment in Paraguay as being "in some respects the triumph of humanity.[iii]"

When they learned that the wild Indians had been brought into such a state of civilisation under Communism, that they not only grew the raw materials for textile fabrics but actually wove them into garments, the pioneers felt that at least as much could be accomplished by highly intelligent Australians. And since the untutored Indians, in their far inland wildernesses, could construct well-built towns, surrounded by smiling fields, abounding in every kind of produce, how much greater things might be done by Anglo-Saxons within a few miles of a railway, shops and civilisation generally.

It is interesting to note, in passing, how the citizens of the 'Christian Republic' dealt with that perplexing problem of Socialism —"When all are equal how will it be decided who is to be a dust-man, and who a magistrate?"

"In each settlement there were two schools, the one for the elements of letters, the other for the dance and music," Chateaubriand tells us, "As soon as a child reached the age of seven, the priests studied his character. If he seemed fitted to mechanical employment they put him in one of the settlement's workshops, and, in that, moreover to which inclination directed him. He became a gold-smith, gilder, watchmaker, etc. The young people who preferred agriculture were enrolled among the labourers, and those who retained some of the love of roaming characteristic of their old life followed the herds."

"The ground was divided into several lots, and each family cultivated one of the lots for its needs. There was also a public field, known as 'God's possession.' The fruit of these communal lands was destined to supplement bad harvests and maintain the widows, the orphans and the sick."

"The magistrates were named by the general assemblage of citizens, but only from a list formed by the missionaries. ... As suggested by Plato, the missionaries used to set aside the children who gave indication of genius in order to initiate them into the arts and sciences; it was from this excellent group that the priests, magistrates, and heroes of the fatherland would one day emerge."

This nominal distinction of rank between members of the community does not appear to have bred ill-feeling since duties were assigned without distinction of person. A Protestant critic of the Jesuits admits:
"In all their duties the missionaries took the lead, nobles by birth and learned men fresh from the universities of Europe, might be seen acting as shepherds, masons, carpenters, and carrying on all manner of common trades, for the purpose of teaching and stimulating the natives, who gazed with confused bewilderment at the strange spectacle. The result of all these precautions and efforts to maintain a community of goods may be summed up in a few words. 'The Indians- are poor, and yet lack nothing. They maintain among themselves perfect equality, which is the strongest support of union and public tranquility."

Many writers insist that the civilisation which the Jesuits so successfully established was used principally for their own gain, and that the bulk of the goods produced were exported to enrich the coffers of their militant order. If that were so it merely proves that the wealth producing capabilities of the community were even greater than appeared on the surface, and that had there been no such leakages the happy Paraguayans would have been more prosperous still. Since it was possible for the "priest-ridden savages" to do so well, it seemed reasonable to suppose that the emancipated 'New Australians' — having thrown of all superstitious shackles — would do still better.

When they reached the magnificent property known as the Lowry estate, which Dr. Lopez proposed to put freely at their disposal, the prospectors' last doubt vanished, and they at once decided that this was the ideal site for Lane's experiment. As the bona-fides, both of the prospectors and of the Paraguayan Government has been called in question, most unjustly, by critics who know nothing of the country, it is worth while noting that in an official report on 'New Australia,' from the British Legation in Buenos Aires, the concession is thus described: "The settlement is situated on some rising ground and looks over a long stretch of pasture land bounded by forest and dotted by clumps of trees. There is something very English in the landscape, and this is true of other parts of Paraguay. It appeared to my companion and myself that the Government had treated the association very well, not only as regards the quantity, but as regards the quality of the land conceded. The association has secured 100 leagues (they have already received the titles for 67 leagues) of what I believe to be the best land in Paraguay. It is well-watered and well-wooded, and in Paraguay wherever there is forest the soil is very fertile, and will grow almost anything. The pasture land is also excellent and I was informed, on good authority, that the district now occupied by the association was requisitioned by the Dictator Lopez during the Paraguayan war, for 50,000 head of cattle — and met the demand."

The conditions of settlement were generous in the extreme. The Government undertook: — (1) to hand over to the New Australia Association, for bona-fide settlement, one hundred leagues of land, free of all charges, including survey, stamps and transfer fees; (2) to admit tools, furniture, clothes, arms and ammunition, seeds and anything else the immigrants chose to bring, or desired to import later, for their own use, duty free; (3) to give the immigrants free railway transport for themselves and their possessions to the nearest point of their concession; (4) to grant local autonomy, with no responsibility except to the Central Government.

In return the Association were only required to establish 800 families upon the land, within four years.

To this proposal the prospectors hastened to agree and a legal document was drawn up embodying its terms. After cabling the news to Australia Leek and Walker remained to make arrangements for receiving the first settlers, while Saunders returned to Australia in the character of Joshua to make the joyful announcement. "The land which we passed through to search it, is an exceeding good land."

The following are the principal clauses from the prospectors' long and glowing report:

"Paraguay has no sea-board. The capital, Asuncion, is situated about 1000 miles from Buenos Ayres, by river, in lat. 25. Its communication with other countries is by rivers, the Paraguay and the Parana. The Paraguay river is navigable to Asuncion for vessels drawing 9ft. to 10ft., all the year round, and for about 1000 miles further for vessels drawing 6ft. all seasons of the year. There are three regular steamship lines to Asuncion which run weekly boats. Schooners sail right up the river, as it is miles wide nearly all the way. Enquiries made among many people show that Paraguay, while sadly in need of land workers since the war of '65, is not a disturbed country. Its constitution has remained unchanged since 1870, there is universal suffrage, religious liberty and an Elected Congress and President. It does not have revolutions. We cannot speak too well of the manner in which all classes treated us. Foreigners are protected by their nationality from military conscription.

"The site selected and which has been secured is situated near a place called Villa Rica, and within fifteen miles of railway communication. It is on the Tebicuari river which runs through it, passing under the railway line, about twenty miles from Villa Rica towards Asuncion. The river is a nice stream and clear as crystal. It is navigable to our land by boats or rafts, pushed by poles, while for export we could hardly get better convenience, very useful where there is a good deal of valuable timber. We have thus rail and water to our door. Numerous smaller streams whose water runs all the year round, a fact somewhat strange to most Australians, are on our land, affording any amount of constant water power when required.

"No one that we have met questions the fertility of the soil, and it is the best watered country that we have ever seen. The high lands, or forest lands, are generally of a red sandy or loamy description covered with heavy timber of different kinds. There are many useful woods, mostly hard-woods; but there are some soft woods, also cedar. There is timber fit for anything. Our land is mostly this timber land with red, loamy soil, though there is some of it clear camp land.

"All foreigners agree that it is remarkably healthy and that sickness is scarce. It is free from fevers and such like diseases generally met with in warm climates. There is a little malarial fever sometimes among the native population in the low-lying districts close to the big rivers. But this is in a great measure due to the way in which they live and to the lowness and dampness of the soil in those localities. Villa Rica is said to be remarkably healthy. An Englishman, Dr. Botrill, who is a London hospital physician of some repute and who has lived there for some time owing to ill-health, told us he considered it a remarkably healthy place.

"The rainfall is better than it is in most countries, as they are never a whole month without rain in Paraguay, and the heaviest rainfall is in the summer, which is an advantage in a warm climate. It is possible to raise crops of some kind during all seasons of the year.

"The principal things grown are tobacco, sugar-cane, cotton, maize, coffee, grapes, peaches, oranges, lemons and vegetables of all descriptions. Tobacco is the principal article exported at present, and grows splendidly.

"The disadvantages are not having a good local market and the density of the timber on a greater portion of the land which requires a lot of labour to clear. Of these disadvantages the question of local market, so important to the individual settlers, is not of importance with our settlement methods. Timber is in great demand in the Argentine, and there is a very large saw mill at Villa Rica. There is a certain market for various products in Buenos Aires and Monte Video. The distance to London by water is only twenty-six days from Asuncion, much nearer than any part of Australasia. A great deal of the timber cleared would be useful and saleable at once. We will thus be sure of a certain remuneration for the labour of clearing.

"Paraguay, like every other South American country, is no good for those who work for wages. For those who have land to work on for themselves, however, it is good. You sometimes hear of a family supporting itself, and keeping a cow on an acre of land, but you seldom see it. Neither of us ever did until we went to Paraguay. It is nothing uncommon there. The great settlement advantage is that from the beginning we can get fresh food, fruit and vegetables close at hand until we grow our own. We think that an acre cleared in Paraguay will produce as much as two in most other countries. We feel confident that with enough capital to land, sufficient tools and food to keep us say 18 months, it will only be sheer laziness if we don't prosper. And starvation is impossible."

CHAPTER IV.

SAILING OF THE ROYAL TAR.

The publication of this report produced a profound sensation in Australia. In spite of all that William Lane had said and written about his emigration project there had been a general feeling that he would not really succeed in carrying it through; in fact it was believed by many that the New Australia Co-operative Association was merely some new and ingenious form of 'land-swindle.' But when it was known that he had actually obtained a free grant of nearly six hundred square miles of land on which to found his settlement, public incredulity gave way to consternation.

Long before this Lane had thoroughly prepared his ground. Thousands of honest workers, who were actually more prosperous than their "mates" in other countries, had been hypnotised by a long course of red-hot Socialism into thinking themselves unhappy martyrs to the capitalistic system. In the same number of the New Australia Journal which contained the prospectors' report he issued a final manifesto and a strong appeal:

"Immense populations are being crowded into the ugly streets of unhealthy towns, where they are handy for the system. In the farming districts men and women sweat their lives out for the mortgagee. In the West men live a peg lower than blackfellows, without wives, without homes, with little but drinking and gambling to make a change in their empty lives. The small shopkeepers, the small employers, are little better off. And it is so hard to live that we are all being driven to do mean and dishonourable things in order to get an advantage over some poor struggling fellow-creature, who is striving to live as we are ourselves. You know it is so. Every man knows it is so. We are going to stop this hateful struggling, this degrading competition, in New Australia".

Now that the opportunity was at hand to put in practice the whole hot gospel of Socialism, Lane's pen became more fiercely inspired than ever.
"Your Labour is a mere 'commodity your life-blood must be sold as so much wood or wool," he wrote, "Yet Labour alone produces wealth. There can be no justice until Labour can work without asking leave of any and without paying profit to any. . . . This ownership which causes misery and vice and poverty and wretchedness unspeakable, all the social evils from which you suffer and from which the world suffers, is a veritable sin. We have lived wickedly in taking part in a system which is wicked and sinful, which is brutish, not human, selfish not loving."

Lane had another motive in addition to securing the mere material prosperity of those who accompanied him. He believed that the success of his venture would pave the way at once to the realisation of 'Socialism in our time.' "Industrial reorganization," he asserted, "must be pioneered by those who know it to be possible before faith and hope can come to the millions who are really groping blindly in the dark. New Australia is such a pioneering movement. Without injuring any, without abandoning any principle, without threatening violence, or preaching submission, it will prove to the workers of the world the value of working co-operatively, each for all and all for each, under conditions which secure for everyone the right to work and happiness in living. The happiness of its members will excite the emulation of the vast multitude whom no theories can reach; its methods, tried and proved, will be a sure guide for others to follow; and the influence of its example will aid tremendously in the peaceful and orderly settlement of the social problem which now threatens civilisation with utter destruction."

The effect of this manifesto coupled with the prospectors' report, was electrical. With passionate eagerness thousands clamoured for a place in the great exodus, convinced that worry, and want, and social inequality would have no place in New Australia. But many, like the young man in the Scriptures, 'went away sorrowful' when they heard the financial conditions. Since equality was the very essence of Lane's scheme it was ordained that every man who joined must put into the common treasury every penny he possessed. Businesses, houses, land, all must be sold and the proceeds handed over. As a mark of bona-fides every male member on joining the Association was required to pay down the sum of £10, which was non-returnable, and before he could set sail from Australia each man must make up his contribution to a minimum of £60. "We only fix a minimum from a necessity, so that there may be no danger of failure, and all in the settlement must start on the same footing. If any man who wishes to join has more he must throw in all he has. We do not want anybody who does not feel ready to go 'mates' with everybody else that joins. Women are not required to pay anything."

Of course there were many who wished to join the New Australia movement who did not possess so much as sixty pounds. But it was pointed out to them that they need not leave with the first party:
"Those who cannot join at once will have a motive for saving by joining, will be encouraged to make a long pull by the knowledge that their comrades are at work, building up the settlement and waiting to greet them when they come."

The touching confidence in his leadership which the bushmen displayed affected Lane himself to strong emotion:
"It brings tears to my eyes," he once wrote to a friend, "to see how my bushmen trust me, how they hand me over their hard earned money without a doubt or question as to the use I make of it. I would rather die than betray such trust."

Certainly nothing was further from Lane's mind, for he was personally the soul of honour. But what a responsibility to undertake! Did it never occur to him, that, just possibly his theories were wrong, that there might be some small error in his calculations? Apparently not, for he let people sell up their homes without a protest. Having proved his own belief in the movement by throwing in the £1000 he had saved during many years of arduous labour, it did not trouble him in the slightest when business men sold their shops for a song and selectors abandoned their improvements — fruits of the toil of years — to follow him. Perhaps the most remarkable thing about the movement was that it was by no means confined to the poorest class of worker. Several tradesmen contributed from £400 to £1500 in cheerful confidence that they sustained no loss, since within a few years every member of the Socialist band would be rich, in happiness and material comfort, beyond the dreams of avarice.

Of course the Australian Press was not silent about the folly of the undertaking. All, save the Socialist journals, joined in denouncing it as madness. Although it was one of the principles of the Association to recognise marriage, some realised only too well the fact that Socialism and conventional morality are absolutely incompatible:
"I would rather see my daughter or sister take a leap off the North Head than have her join this party," one far-sighted correspondent wrote to the Sydney Daily Telegraph. "Little do

they imagine the sorrow in store for them and I hope that it may not yet be too late to interfere to save them from their fate."

But it was too late. New Australia had caught on, not with the scum of the slums of whom the cities would have been well rid, but with the pick of the working men of Queensland and New South Wales. "There is no denying the fact that the New Australia movement is calling from the ranks of Australian labour many of its best and most worthy representatives," said the Sydney Daily Telegraph sorrowfully.

When the seriousness of the situation was realised, when it was known that thousands were prepared to follow provided that the first contingent 'made good' and reported favourably upon the settlement, a strong appeal was made to the patriotism of the men in the movement. It was suggested that the Government should assign some choice territory in Australia for the great experiment in Socialism rather than that so many sturdy citizens should desert the country. But Lane made short work of such objections; like other honest Socialists he pointed out that Socialism and patriotism have nothing at all in common.

"What is one country more than another to the man whose whole life is one of toil and poverty, and what does Australia do more than England does, or any other countries do, for the workers?" he demanded in the New Australia Journal. "The Labour movement is world-wide. It is not a local question nor a national question, but a life question. If the workers have not yet learnt this they will simply suffer more until they learn it, perhaps too late. It is here, as everywhere else, the landless have no rights, the poor have no country except in name. In this New Australia movement we exchange empty patriotism to a country in which we have no share, for the solid possession of a great tract of good land, secured under terms which could not possibly be secured here. On this land we can build the settlement we seek, can exert our Labour as will satisfy our needs, can produce not only food and clothing and buildings, but articles to export in exchange for what we must import, can have plenty and be happy, and teach the world a lesson. It is our opportunity. Are we not to take it? Shall a great movement drop because some are still foolish enough to mistake the real needs of Labour?"

The money rolled in so fast that it was necessary to establish a company to take legal control of it. For form's sake 'The New Australia Co-operative Colonisation Society' was duly registered as a company, with a capital of £20,000 in £10 shares, on which, however, it was stipulated that no interest should be paid. The directors were so convinced that the movement would be a permanent thing that they would not hear of chartering a ship to take the first party to South America. In 'Freeland,' Dr. Hertzka represents his ideal community as requiring its own fleet of noble steamers to bring the constant stream of recruits from the effete old capitalistic countries; the New Australians aimed at following that plan, and, to begin with, paid £1200 for a sailing ship, of 600 tons, the 'Royal Tar'. By many members of the Association it was considered an ill-omened thing to embark in a boat with the words 'Royal' as part of its name; they were extremely anxious to re-christen it, in fact : but it was found that there would be many formalities to be complied with and they decided to let the name remain.

In connection with the 'Royal Tar's' first voyage there was so much friction between the leaders of the movement and the authorities, that the boat was delayed for two months after its advertised sailing date, during which time the passengers, having sold their homes, were compelled to remain on shore at the expense of the Association. To this day many New Australians assert that the vexatious delay was deliberately planned by the Government to damage the movement, but the fact was that the shipping officials were anxious that nothing should be left undone to safeguard the emigrants lives. The first delay was due to an intimation that the barge would not be allowed to sail until she had been fitted with a new mainmast, new cable and anchor, and three large new boats; the second was caused by the discovery that the vessel had been provisioned for little more than the bare time the voyage was expected to take — the authorities naturally enough insisting that sufficient stores should be shipped to last, if necessary, for 130 days; the third was occasioned by the fact that the vessel had not paid its harbour dues — an exaction insisted on strictly in advance in the case of Socialists.

At last, however, all formalities were complied with and the boat was ready to sail. On the eve of its departure a great farewell demonstration was held at Sydney at which the speakers were Members of Parliament and prominent Labour leaders. There was something ominous in the words "for the present" on which emphasis was laid in the following official resolution, passed with acclamation by the assembly: "That this meeting of New South Wales citizens whilst deeply regretting the loss to Australia of so many co-workers in the cause of reform, believes that the efforts of the New Australia pioneers to establish in another land a co-operative settlement in which there shall be work for all and overwork for none, and where every man and woman shall have the liberty to live under fair conditions, will prove eminently successful and of great future benefit to those who are compelled for the present to remain in Old Australia: and further desires to express its indignation at the action of the authorities in impeding the departure of peaceful Australian people."

In their enthusiasm the local organisers in each district refused to allow their followers to take with them any but the most essential personal possessions. The men sold their saddles and the women their sewing-machines, things which would have been invaluable in their new homes. Everything was sacrificed for what it would fetch, and the money put into the common fund. The keynote of the movement was faith in one's fellow man, but, as in the case Ananias and Sapphira, there were some who betrayed the trust reposed in them, and kept back part of the price. Long before the boat was permitted to sail contingents from Queensland, South Australia, and Tasmania reached Sydney, where they had to camp in the open for weeks. When at last they were permitted to go on board the scene was of the most remarkable description, a long stream of pilgrims wending their way to the ship, carrying all their worldly possessions upon their shoulders. Among other strange things embarked was a steam hammer, which one of the enthusiasts felt sure would be useful in the primaeval forest: "There were men and women and children," wrote a lively journalist, "boxes, portmanteaux, and tins; men struggled along the road with massive domestic cargoes on their shoulders, women struggled with their infants, and the infants struggled with each other."

Some may have felt misgivings when the final moment of departure came but not so William Lane. His faith in the triumph of his cause never wavered.

"What do we expect ? This:— for every man the right to work, to every man friendship and justice, for every man and woman a fair share of the result of common work, for each and all the opportunity to marry and have comfortable homes and to live without fear and to fill life with the pleasures and joys that can be for each where all are content to labour honestly, for the children the healthy rearing which is every child's right.

"That is what we expect, and what we can be sure of, for Labour never fails to produce plenty where it is able to work, and the labourers are only struggling and poverty-stricken where conditions block Labour and deprive the worker of the fruit of his labouring."

The hopes of all on board were high as the vessel set sail from Sydney, though some of the women gazed back wistfully at the shore ... for it is no light thing to tear up old associations by the roots and to say 'Farewell forever' to the land of one's birth. However, each endeavoured to suppress any outward sign of such regrets, for were they not about to take part in a fuller, freer life, a hundred times happier than any they had hitherto experienced? Were they not about to teach the world a lesson?

CHAPTER V.

A MATTER OF MORALS.

Socialists are not fond of talking about New Australia, but when they do its distressing failure is accounted for by asserting either (1) that the country to which Lane's party migrated was unsuitable for white men to settle in, or (2) that the party itself was made up of visionaries and work-shy individuals without the necessary energy and experience for pioneering. The first of these statements is confuted in advance by the testimony of the experienced prospectors themselves, and by the fact that other Britishers and Germans live healthily and are doing very well in Paraguay; to dispose of the second it is only necessary to quote from the Sydney Bulletin — a journal which was utterly opposed to the movement and tried hard to dissuade the public from joining it — the following unsolicited testimonial:
"The New Australian contingent contains the best material for such an experiment the world could furnish, perhaps. The work that lies in front of them provided they are allowed to go squarely at it, and it proves to be worth doing, is just the sort they have been used to. There are few town-dwellers among the first batch, and the majority of those who are now rolling their swags in Queensland and South Australia with a view to the second, are of the bush. They have been trained in the tasks of settlement. Tank-sinkers, shearers, bush-carpenters, station-hands, with artisans used to the rough-and-tumble life of Australia will not be easily knocked out."

If picked men such as these, under an absolutely honest leader, failed to 'make good' in their attempt it is quite evident that the general public, including the unskilled and incompetent, would make a far worse hash of a similar experiment.

Nothing could exceed the enthusiasm with which the party commenced to lead the ideal life. Since social inequality was swept away there was not a 'Mister' on board the Royal Tar; everyone was 'Jack,' 'Tom' and 'Charlie,' or 'Nell,' 'Mary' and 'Sue.' An urchin of ten was entitled to address William Lane as 'Billy,' though the leader of the movement was more generally referred to as 'King Billy.'

A good opportunity for the display of brotherly feeling was afforded when the berths came to be allotted. A vessel of less than 600 tons provided remarkably little cabin accommodation for nearly 250 persons, among whom there were 60 single men, and a number of single girls, in addition to the 'grass widowers,' married couples and children. Those who had seen the tiny ship in Sydney Harbour were puzzled to know how so many persons could be stowed inside her, unless they were stacked like cargo or chained in densely packed rows as in the bad old days of the slave trade. But there were a number of bush carpenters among the pioneers, who had exercised their skill in turning every inch of the deep hold to full account. In the forecastle triple tiers of berths ran round the bulkheads to accommodate the single men, the intervening space being filled with tables which could be hauled out of the way overhead when not required. In the ship's waist the married couples and children were so closely packed that the Sydney Telegraph remarked:

"Between decks where the emigrants will live, and eat and sleep, and have their two months' being are simply a mass of plain deal. Apart from the curtains to the cabins of the married women and the single girls, the place is destitute of those accessories which add to the pleasures of life. It is a wilderness of bare boards with no entrance for the sun's rays except what may be afforded by the dead-lights. Indeed a voyage in the 'Royal Tar' in dirty weather round Cape Horn would be calculated to drive anyone but an enthusiast to the verge of gibbering lunacy."

There was very little comfort on board the Royal Tar, except in the after deck cabin where Captain Logan and his wife and daughter stayed. Lane set an example of unselfishness by choosing for his own use one of the smallest and worst placed cabins on the boat, and most of his flock good-temperedly accepted the positions allotted to them, though it was arranged that lots should be drawn to settle who should have the best places if any dispute arose. For the first few days, however, till the party had found their sea-legs in fact, all was perfect peace. Such was the anxiety to be good Socialists that there was keen competition for the privilege of undertaking the most menial tasks - William Lane himself took his turn in the cook's galley at peeling potatoes. There was not work enough to go round; all were so eager to undertake it. As every old traveller knows there are few more trying things on board ship than squalling infants; in the Royal Tar's packed interior such sounds were peculiarly distracting but even the confirmed bachelor comrades at first pretended to like it. At least a dozen people were always willing to take the naughty child from its harassed mother's hands.

Unhappily, however, this beautiful spirit did not last long. Though all were theoretically equal it was found absolutely necessary that some should give, while others should receive, orders. Though all were entitled to an equal voice in the Association's affairs it was not considered practicable to navigate the ship by vote of the majority! Just as the experienced skipper claimed the right of dictating to everybody on matters which concerned the safety of the ship, so Lane insisted on caring for its morals.

Now this question of morals is one about which modern Socialist writers are most wary in admitting their principles. In the old days 'Free Love' was boldly proclaimed as an essential condition of Socialism, but nowadays, to avoid scaring off the timid semi-converts — the Christian Socialists and so on — great care is taken to relegate this phase of Socialism to the background. As Mr. H. G. Wells confesses, so far as English and American Socialism is concerned, the assault on the family "has displayed a quite extraordinary instinct for taking cover."[iv] Nevertheless that assault upon the family is as true to-day as ever; the chief difference between the views of modern Socialists like Mr. H. G. Wells, and those of the "Palaeo-Socialists " (as he describes Godwin and Mary Wollstonecraft, Shelley and Harriet, and even Mr. Belfort Bax) appears to be that the former qualifies the proposals of the latter on the subject of Free Love by a system of State eugenics.

English Socialists to-day still stand where their Continental brethren stood when the Socialist Alliance of Geneva resolved: "The Alliance declares itself atheist, it demands the abolition of all worship, the substitution of science for faith, and of Divine justice for human justice, the abolition of marriage so far as it is a political, religious, judicial, or civil institution."

Mr. Belfort Bax points out the logic of the position in his 'Ethics of Socialism'[v]:
"The present marriage system is bound up in the general supposition of the economic dependence of the woman on the man, and the consequent necessity for his making provision for her, which she can legally enforce. This basis would disappear with the advent of Social economic freedom, and no binding contract would be necessary between the parties as regards

livelihood, while property in children would cease to exist."

In Belfort Bax, we find, "Marriage is to give place to kindly and human relations between the sexes."

It is interesting to note with what heat leading Socialist writers deny that they are tainted with views similar to those stated above. In 'Socialism and the Family,', Mr. H. G. Wells professes himself hotly indignant that the Daily Express should suggest that he and others were involved "in teaching Free Love to respectable working men."

What then does he teach? He says:
"Socialism involves the responsible citizenship of women, their economic independence of men and all the personal freedom that follows that, it intervenes between the children and the parents, claiming to support them, protect them, and educate them for its own ampler purposes. Socialism in fact is the State family. The old family of 'the private individual must vanish before it, just as the old water works of private enterprise, or the old gas company. They are incompatible with it."

When some critic suggested that he desired to reduce humanity to the condition of a stud farm, Mr. Wells complained bitterly of that individual's 'thick-headedness' and strove to remove the bad impression by declaring that Socialism would insist on marriage 'under conditions.' But in the following passage he makes it clear that, by 'marriage' he means a good deal less than the binding tie which all save savage races now insist upon.

"Socialism does not present any theory whatever about the duration of marriage. . . . The State is not urgently concerned with these questions. So long as a marriage contract provides for the health and sanity of the contracting parties, and for their proper behaviour so far as their off-spring need it, the demands of the Community as the guardian of the children, are satisfied. That certainly would be the minimum marriage, the State marriage, and I, for my own part, would exact nothing more in the legal contract. But a number of more representative Socialists than I are for a legally compulsory life marriage. Some — but they are mostly of the older, less definite, Social Democratic teaching — are for a looser tie."

But "the older, less definite, Social Democratic Teaching" makes a far more popular appeal to the masses, whose votes will control the Socialistic State, than any other version of the ' creed.' If so refined a man as Mr. H. G. Wells asks no more than that legal unions shall endure until the children are just old enough for the State "to intervene and support them," is it not certain that the unrefined mob will demand still less? Is it not fair to assume that the loosest form of the 'looser tie' will be the maximum enforced in his nightmare society?

The plain truth is that, as clearly stated in 'Socialism,' by William Morris and Belfort Bax;
"Under a Socialistic system contracts between individuals could be free and unforced by the Community. This would apply to the marriage contract as well as others, and it would become a matter of simple inclination. . . . Nor would a truly enlightened public opinion freed from mere theological views as to chastity insist on the permanently binding nature,"

This matter of morals was bound to cause William Lane acute anxiety, since he was aware that previous attempts to realise the Socialist dream of an ideal State had broken down from this very cause. Though the leading Socialists agree that marriage is a ridiculous institution, as husband and father Lane personally had the greatest respect for it. But he had no guarantee that the sixty bachelors in his party shared this sentiment. Was it not probable that, together with the Socialist creed he had himself disseminated, they had imbibed the logical notion that "communism of goods leads as a necessary consequence to communism of wives, children and parents?"

Though he had provided for communism of goods and communism of children Lane was determined to preserve the conventional relations between the sexes and had framed a regulation to that effect. It therefore gave him some anxiety when he discovered a tendency among some of his followers to relieve the tedium of the voyage by a little harmless flirtation. He feared in fact that it might be said of his experiment as it was of Brook Farm; "They did not seek to interfere with marriage, nay, they guarded that holy state with reverence, yet the spirit of fraternal association was found to weave itself, with infinite subtleties, into the most tender relations of man and woman. Fear came into the common dwelling."

One of the first dissensions arose from the women's objection to remain in the stuffy atmosphere of the holds, below the water line, from sunset till sunrise. It was not much fun for either sex to spend many hours cooped up in the dim light provided by a smoking hurricane lamp, and, in consequence, many elected to spend the greater part of the night on deck, discussing the beautiful principles of Socialism with some kindred spirit under the open vault of heaven. If that kindred spirit happened to be of the opposite sex, there could be no logical objection, since sex equality under Socialism implies the permissibility of the warmest comradeship between any man or woman in spite of the fact that either or both may happen to be married.

This was a question, however, about which Lane did not profess to be logical. He only believed in liberty, equality and fraternity within certain limits and so issued a decree forbidding members of the gentler sex henceforth to appear on deck after sunset.

That was a fatal error: on the first night when it was put in force the ladies held an indignation meeting, and many of the most straight laced among them agreed that it was an intolerable insult, as well as an unwarrantable act of tyranny to coop them up in such a fashion. Worse still, it was discovered that William Lane, while taking counsel with certain of the married women, had not consulted any maiden ladies before issuing his decree, although several of the latter were full-fledged members of the Association in their own right.

Breaking out into active rebellion they stormed the hatchway and reminded their leader that they had an equal say with him in the conduct of affairs, and had as much right to order him to his cabin as he had to order them.

One indignant young lady, stepping over to the notice board, tore down William Lane's notice before his face and danced upon it. Just to assert their rights, some of the married women openly incited the younger girls to disobey, and a number made a point at once of spending the greater part of the night on deck in future, to prove their independence. As a matter of fact, however, the ladies were quite mistaken in supposing that they had yet any right to a voice in the control of things.

Before leaving Australia Lane had arranged that the 'Constitution' was suspended, and that he was to act (in association with three staunch henchmen on whose support he could rely) as Director for the first two years, with power to dictate internal arrangements. It is true that a two-thirds majority vote could displace him, but, as he held proxies for all members of the Association still in Australia, his single vote constituted a majority.

But it is one thing to possess nominal power and quite another to be able to enforce it. When William Lane's authority was flouted a general meeting was called to decide: "whether the authority of the Chairman shall be respected?"

Unfortunately Lane was too seasick to attend, and so, unswayed by his personal influence, the majority passed a resolution declaring that he was not to be obeyed. To this William Lane retorted by resigning office, whereupon even his bitterest opponents realised that they had gone too far and a second general meeting passed a resolution requesting him to reconsider his decision. Finally William Lane called a third general meeting and played so well upon the emotions of his erring flock that they passed a vote of confidence in his rule without a single dissentient. The net result of the whole affair was simply to confirm William Lane in his authority as an absolute dictator.

CHAPTER VI.

WHO WILL DO THE SCAVENGING?

To many of the pioneers it came as something of a shock to realize that they were to be subject to a benevolent despotism, until such time as the second contingent arrived at New Australia, and a quite unreasonable feeling sprang up that Lane had got the better of them — unreasonable because they were supposed fully to understand the arrangement before embarking. But it is a curious trait of the Socialist rank and file that they are quite willing blindly to accept the promises of their leaders without wanting to know, in detail, how much individual liberty will be sacrificed in the process of carrying them out.

Before the voyage was half over an awkward split had occurred in the ranks, and the Utopian party were sharply divided into two factions — those who believed in Lane and were prepared to support him through thick and thin, and those who were already more or less dissatisfied with his leadership. The latter section soon got into such a state of mind that they were prepared to believe themselves slighted and victimised whenever the shadow of an excuse arose. A good opportunity to feel aggrieved was presented when Lane took stock of his resources and began to apportion tasks among his followers.

While on his recruiting mission in Australia Lane once explained; "At New Australia a man may produce a loaf of bread or a painting, but there will be no difference in the remuneration of his labour."
"Yes," interrupted a practical minded inquirer, "but who is to do the washing up?"

Now this question "Who is to do the washing up?" is another of those practical problems which Socialist theorists exercise a good deal of ingenuity in avoiding.

In 'Merrie England,' Mr, Robert Blatchford devotes a portion of Chapter XXIV to some clever circumlocution round and about the query: 'Under Socialism: Who will do the disagreeable work? Who will do the scavenging?'
"We have heard a good deal of more or less clumsy ridicule at the expense of the Socialist. We have heard learned and practical men laugh them to scorn; we have seen their claims and their desires and their theories held up to derision. But can anyone imagine a sight more contemptible or more preposterous than that of a civilised and wealthy nation coming to a halt in its march of progress for fear of disturbing the minds of the scavengers?"

It will not be the scavengers alone, however, but the 'under dogs' in every calling — at least one hundred times as numerous as the 'top dogs' — who will cry "Halt" when jobs come to be distributed. When all are equal and all clamour to be artists, or inventors, or managers, or, at the very least, foremen, how will the difficulty be met? In his section on the subject Mr. Blatchford calls on the shades of Cromwell, of Langton, of Washington, and of Hampden; he ridicules the noble lords of the British Parliament; he compares the Conservative to Mrs. Partington with her mop, but he does not answer his own question. Instead he refers the reader back to an earlier chapter, and to Mrs. Besant's paper on 'The Organisation of Society.' Dealing with the latter first, the reader finds that Mrs. Besant merely re-states the problem as follows; "There are unpleasant and indispensable forms of labour which one would imagine, can attract none — mining, sewer-cleaning, etc. These might be rendered more attractive by making the hours of labour in them much shorter than the normal working day of pleasanter occupations. . . Further, much of the most disagreeable and laborious work might be done by machinery, as it would be now if it were not cheaper to exploit a helot class. When it became illegal to send small boys up chimneys, chimneys did not cease to be swept, a machine was invented for sweeping them."

Quite so, but for the present there are numerous unpleasant tasks which must be performed by manual labour; who will do them now? It is not courageous of Mr. Blatchford to hide behind a lady, whose not very practical argument reminds one of Dr. Johnson's suggestion to the weary postman who had still two miles to walk to deliver a single letter ("Why don't you put a stamp on it and post it?" enquired the doctor).

"For an answer to this question I must refer you back to my chapter on 'Socialism and Slavery,'" says Mr. Blatchford. Referring back, the reader finds Herbert Spencer attacked for describing Socialism as 'The Coming Slavery.' "Mr, Spencer's idea appears to be that under Socialism the State would compel men to work against their will, or to work at occupations uncongenial to them. This is a mistake. The State would not compel any man to work. It would only enable all men to work and to live in peace and comfort by their labour."

Next he attacks Ingersoll for saying:
"Socialism destroys the family and sacrifices the liberties of all. If the Government is to provide work it must decide for the worker what he must do etc. Is it possible to conceive of a despotism beyond this? The human race cannot afford to exchange its liberty for any possible comfort."

Mr. Blatchford, after roundly abusing both critics, defiantly asserts, "when the State found work it would not decide what each man must do. You will ask me how a Socialist State would apportion the work, I ask you how the work is apportioned now?"

It is a time-honoured debating trick to put off one awkward question by propounding another. In that device Mr. Blatchford takes refuge here, and devotes five pages of close print to abuse of present conditions, without shedding the least light upon the nature of his proposed remedy. The question "Under Socialism, who would do the unpleasant work?" remains unanswered still.

In 'New Worlds for Old' Mr. H. G. Wells sets himself a similar poser, "How will you Socialists get the right man in the right place for the work that has to be done? How will you arrange promotion? How will you determine who is to engage in Historical research in the Bodleian, and who is to go out seaward in November and catch mackerel?"
The question is admirably stated, and the earnest inquirer looks for a direct answer from a writer who is habitually frank. He is, however, once more disappointed. "Through-out the rest of this book I hope that the reader will be able to see growing together in this aspect and then in that, in this and that suggestion, the complex solution of this complex system of difficulties," says Mr. Wells.

Then, like the rest, he darts away at a tangent. The most expert solver of Baconian ciphers might search the succeeding 244 pages in vain for the slightest clue to Mr. Wells' 'complex solution.' Like all the theorists Mr. Wells fails utterly to explain how the common work of the practical problems of everyday life will be grappled with under Socialism.

Yet the solution is by no means so complex as Mr. Wells asserts. In fact the answer is so simple that a child can understand it: "In the Socialist State the friends of the administration will get the pleasant jobs and their critics will be set to do the scavenging"

As a matter of fact that precise question, "who is to do the washing up?" had already caused a certain amount of feeling among the men and women on the Royal Tar. Of course there were no regular stewards, and the task of waiting upon and washing up after the 250 persons who sat down at meals had to be apportioned by rota. But what if one day's washers-up did not "feel up to the mark," or "refused to work beside that woman Susan"? What if the member of the 'Shearers' Union' whose turn it was to scrub decks protested that it was not his trade? Trivial questions, perhaps, but infinitely harder of amicable solution than much bigger ones.

Before the pioneers reached South America it was necessary to appoint foremen for each department of activity in which they would engage on their arrival, and also to assign to each of these the group of men who were to work under him. Before sailing it had been arranged that such matters of detail would be adjusted by mutual agreement. Nobody foresaw how unlikely it was that an individual, who was quite famous on the Downs as a crack shearer, would consent to be anything less than a foreman, although there would be no shearing to be done at New Australia, and he was quite without experience of any other occupation. Then again, before any progress could be made with agriculture big clearings would require to be made in the primeval forest — but there were no members of a 'Tree-fellers Union' aboard; to whom should this excessively hard work be allotted?

Who, on the other hand, would be lucky enough to secure such light labour as the secretarial work? And which of the women would have to turn laundress for the benefit of the sixty bachelors on board ?

Those who imagined that such questions as these could be settled in an amicable fashion, without invoking the arbitrary authority of the director were sadly undeceived. Ultimately, of course, the matter was temporarily decided, and a list drawn up assigning the roundest possible pegs to the squarest holes and vice-versa, with the inevitable result that fully one-third of the Utopians nursed in their breasts a conviction that they were being unjustly treated.

"No matter what was proposed by this committee, or, for that matter, by any committee," Mrs, William Lane herself complained, "a large section of the members were sure to flout it with a long string of captious objections."

The mere statement of two distinct types of grievance will show that Solomon himself could not have given universal satisfaction under such conditions, (1) As responsible head of the organisation William Lane could not possibly appoint as his chief foremen individuals who were in open rebellion against him. Yet if those rebels happened to be particularly competent men how could they fail to believe that they were being victimised? (2) Though all were theoretically equal, it would have been contrary to human nature if the few who had contributed large sums to the common fund had not felt that the Association was in their debt, and that they had a special right to 'soft jobs' and a share in the administration. But — to say nothing of the fact that ex-shopkeepers are of less use than ex-navvies in such work as forest-clearing — it would have been fatal to the movement for such undemocratic claims to be conceded. Nevertheless, since human nature is human nature, how could a business man who had put in several hundred pounds fail to feel aggrieved when he was instructed to form one of an ordinary labouring gang, bossed by a brawny artisan who had only contributed his bare minimum to the enterprise?

Quite apart from the causes of quarrel between a section of the New Australians and their leader, further acute dissension broke out among certain of the Socialists themselves over this question of contributions. In the agreement, which all signed before they were admitted to membership, it was laid down, "Every member of the Association, by act of joining the Association agrees to subscribe to the funds of the Association all he may possess when he is finally enrolled," and most had honestly adhered to this arrangement. But some days before the Royal Tar had left Sydney the following paragraph appeared in the Sydney Daily Telegraphy:
"It is stated there is one man among the voyagers who has not staked everything on the success of the new system, but has kept some landed property he possesses in Brisbane as a stand-by in case, at any time, he should want money to return to Queensland."
Naturally those who saw this statement felt incensed against the unknown individual who "had kept back part of the price" and as the voyage proceeded at least half a dozen persons were accused of being the guilty party. Though all hotly denied the accusation the suspicion remained that a few of the Socialists had not burnt their boats like the others, but had merely moored them out of sight where they might be useful for retreat if necessary.

Since the last-moment repairs, alterations, and extra provisioning of the Royal Tar had cost roughly £1200, William

Lane was obliged to embark with only about twenty-five pounds in the exchequer — not nearly sufficient for the party's immediate needs when they reached Monte Video. As some members of the party still had a few odd coins in their possession, it was decided — contrary to Mr. H. G. Wells' belief that "Modern Socialism has no designs upon the money in a man's pocket," —
to take up a final collection of everyone's last halfpenny.

Theoretically, therefore, there was no money on the ship except that in Lane's possession when the New Australians stepped ashore at Monte Video — where the press went into raptures over the looks of the "exceptionally beautiful and comely" Australian women. It soon became evident, however, that a few of the Socialists had indeed retained a private hoard for use in cases of emergency. Their perfidy, already suspected, was proved when a number of them returned to the boat quite expensively intoxicated. Had it not been for the bad impression that such a move would have created in Australia they would doubtless have been expelled at once from the community. Lane shrank from such an extreme for the present, however, and the sinners were let off with a severe reprimand. Mutual recriminations necessarily followed this revelation of bad 'mateship' and the split in the camp was daily widened.

When the necessary funds arrived from Sydney, and the party embarked for the 1300 mile trip up the broad river to Asuncion, another incident, small in itself, stirred up still more ill-feeling. During the wearisome voyage from Australia, of about 60 days, the children had tasted none but the plainest food and their parents were anxious to give them a little treat. Since there was no money available for the purpose, some of them bartered various personal belongings for a barrel of native molasses, which young and old pronounced delicious. But alas one of those in authority declared that the molasses contained a certain percentage of alcohol, and was therefore, according to the strict letter of the New Australian law, prohibited. Disregarding the children's tears, their mothers' protests, and the stronger language of their fathers, the newly elevated officers seized the barrel and heaved it over-board where it could harm the morals of none but the crocodiles.

CHAPTER VI.

THE ARRIVAL IN PARAGUAY.

Asuncion did not very favourably impress Australians accustomed to the splendid buildings of Melbourne and Sydney, though the ruins of many fine structures attested the fact that it was once a busy and prosperous city. But they were charmed by the cordial welcome prepared by the citizens for "the downtrodden Britishers, who loved liberty so much that they had forsaken their distant homes to commence life again in the free air of a South American republic!"

There is probably no country in the world so generous as Paraguay in its treatment of immigrants; on this occasion the authorities— who had lent the Opera House as a temporary home for Lane's party — went even further than usual, for, in the words of a Foreign Office Report, "they knew the merits of the British colonist, and these Australians taken altogether were as fine a set of men and women as it was possible to collect anywhere, and of a stamp much superior to any emigrants yet seen in South America, Everybody who saw them had been struck by their manners, their appearance and their intelligence. . . . They appeared to be, in fact, the very men, representing as they did various trades, and knowing their business well, to help Paraguay on to that road to recovery so earnestly desired."

In the streets and the market place of Asuncion the new-arrivals saw hundreds of merry, white-robed women, hatless, bootless, and clad in a single garment, but few men. Naked children played among the refuse in the gutters, and a few lazy males, wearing long ponchos and enormous spurs, lolled in the shade while the women-folk laboured in the sun. The Australians looked with scorn upon the picturesque drones, but were not ill-pleased at this positive proof of the laziness of Paraguay's inhabitants. "There will be all the more chance for us," said they.

Whatever Lane's personal motives, the thousands whom he had influenced in favour of the New Australia movement were not desirous of joining with the sole notion of teaching the world a lesson. The whole force of the Socialistic appeal to the man in the street lies in its promise of greatly increased material prosperity. The Royal Tar Socialists would never have left their homes without the conviction that the movement was going to pay. It is safe to say that the Socialist creed would make few converts were it not for the dazzling delights which Socialist writers habitually promise. It rarely occurs to the rank and file that the step to State Socialism, once made, would be irrevocable, even if it should lead to absolute ruin.

"They were going to join a little community which would be sure to thrive, and where they and the rest of their family might live together for the rest of their lives in peace and comfort, without any need to separate, without any thought of the morrow. They did not apparently give themselves the trouble to understand the conditions they signed although it was decided that no man, were he to withdraw from the membership, might reclaim his donation after it had been made. It was enough for them what their leaders said," wrote the Second Secretary of the English Legation at Buenos Aires, after he had visited New Australia. The same writer shortly continues:
"Their hopes were raised, their impressions dazzled by accounts which various writers had given of the wealth and fertility of the soil, and by reports which had appeared in a newspaper started by the association called The New Australia. Paraguay was

destined, so they were told, to be selected in the near future as the seat of central government for a Federated Republic of the whole of the South American nations, the greatest republic the world has ever seen, greater by numbers, extent, and riches than either France or North America. The forests abounded in all kinds of valuable woods, there was an unfailing market down the river, and soon the day would come when Europe would have to go to the forests of the Parana and Paraguay for her timber supplies. Cheap lines might easily be built, which would connect the colony with the Amazon and her tributaries, and the largest contracts might be taken and fulfilled. Cotton, rice, and maize might easily be raised and as, in a few years, machinery might be imported, so the place would become a manufacturing as well as an agricultural settlement. Then there was a vast field of enterprise in the improvement of cattle, and what with perfumes and dyes, tobacco and matt, the introduction of which into Europe might be said to be an assured success, it would be a bold man who would dare to predict that failure was in store for the New Australian Colony."

In spite, therefore, of the general feeling of strain there were not yet any secessions. For his part William Lane believed that now the wearisome voyage was over, and there was plenty of hard work to be done, petty squabbles would be forgotten and the joy of working "one for all and all for one" would quickly heal all differences. The essential thing, he realized, was to reach the concession as soon as possible and put an end to some of the friction by separating warring factions as far as possible from one another. As there were certain legal formalities to be complied with, he remained behind in the capital for a few days, and the temporary leadership of the pilgrims devolved upon his principal lieutenants.

It was a great relief to all to feel terra-firma beneath their feet again, and jaded spirits were much refreshed by the keen interest the travellers took in their novel surroundings. When they journeyed on the train which ran three times a week to Caballero, passing magnificent forests and well watered grazing grounds, so different from the dried-up back-blocks of Australia, they waxed enthusiastic over the prospect before them. At Caballero they dumped their possessions into 'caretas' or bullock-carts, and set off over the mountain track, towards the land of promise.

Australians are accustomed to driving bullocks by means of heavy whips, but in Paraguay the goad is used — a long bamboo pole suspended over the animals' backs and provided with a four-inch steel point. At first the pioneers revolted against using this cruel instrument but, finding the bullocks feared nothing else, they soon learned to inflict wicked wounds without a tremor. Their route took them through remarkably picturesque country. Orange trees laden with fruit grew by the way-side, bananas were equally plentiful, pineapples, guavas, and other tropical products were freely at the disposition of the weary travellers. Red and yellow macaw parrots and other birds of gay plumage screamed overhead and butterflies of gorgeous colouring flew in and out among the trees. At first the contemplation of all these natural beauties gave the pioneers considerable satisfaction, but, when the track they were following dwindled suddenly to a narrow footpath, on the outskirts of some dense forest which barred further progress, they began to be perplexed.

"According to the prospectors' report, our concession is within fifteen miles of the railway," they said. "We must surely have come that distance and ought to be within hail of the advance party. What is the meaning of this forest before us, and what has become of the road?"

Their feelings can be better imagined than described when they learned that, while New Australia was within fifteen miles of the line, as the crow flies, the fact that a bottomless morass intervened made It necessary to follow a circuitous route of nearly forty miles. A greater part of this forty mile route moreover, lay through forests into which no bullock cart could penetrate until a 'picada' had been cut. In fact it would take the able-bodied men of the party about three days to hew down sufficient trees on either side of the footpath to permit the broad caretas to pass. Of course this task presented no insuperable difficulties to Australian bushmen accustomed to such work, but the monkeys, which congregated in the tree tops to watch the progress of the work, heard some vivid language used in relation to the prospectors' oversight in omitting such important details from their statement.

There was a further disillusionment in store for the pioneers, on reaching the river Tebicuari, which they had been told flowed through their property. It was naturally a disappointment to men who had imagined that the Tebicuari was one of those noble broad flowing rivers, "they had so often read of, and expected to see in South America, bordered by a dense forest of valuable trees waiting only to be felled, who had thought that they would have been able to start work at once and float the timber down to the nearest market, who had dreamed of a large trade to be established in the near future, and steamers plying busily up and down, to find that the river was merely a stream only navigable by flat-bottomed vessels, and that the settlement was still some twenty miles distant."

Since it is the universal practice in that part of Paraguay to convey squared logs to the saw-mills by bullock cart, the distance of the 'crystal clear river' from their concession made no ultimate difference to the colonists, but they naturally felt that they had been misled in this respect also, and said further harsh things about their unfortunate leader.

The unbridged river was crossed with difficulty, the women and children remaining in the bullock carts which were supported by poles passed between the spokes of the wheels, with projecting ends resting on canoes, the latter being drawn across by the swimming bullocks. Some low-lying mud flats that recent rain had converted into a quagmire were next negotiated. Occasionally the caretas sank to their axles in deep mud holes, and had to be unloaded in the swamp before they could be extricated. At such times millions of mosquitoes descended upon the way-worn travellers and nearly drove them mad. Such little troubles as these are incidental to pioneering the whole world over; it would have been unreasonable for the settlers to expect to find macadamised roads and a light railway already in existence; it was their intention to provide such things by their own energies when a few thousand more of their mates had arrived. At the same time some — among the women particularly — could not help contrasting their many difficulties with the easy progress made by the pioneers in Hertzka's 'Freeland':

"From thence onward it was as if our feet and the feet of our beasts had wings. The pure invigorating air of this beautiful tableland freshened by the winds from the Kenia, the pleasant road over the soft short grass, and the sumptuous and easily obtained provisions, enabled us to make our daily marches longer than we had yet done," relates the author of that fiction, who appears to think that the very mountains will level themselves to mark their approval of a Socialist regime.

As if the difficulties of travel were not enough, matters were made worse by the fact that there was now so much dissension that it was impossible to come to an unanimous agreement upon the smallest matter. When they were nearing the boundaries of their concession, an advance party was sent a few hours ahead of the main body to select a camping ground, and cut forks and ridge poles for the tents. As night was coming on, and there seemed every prospect of a downpour, it was essential that no time should be lost. But nothing could be decided without the formality of a council, and, as usual, opinion was divided. Some favoured a hill on one side of the track, others preferred that on the other. While they argued there came the sudden fall of night, and they were compelled to encamp in the valley. When the caretas arrived, stores were unloaded and tents hurriedly put up, but, alas for their fatal indecision, a storm of wind and rain descended and beat furiously upon them in their unsheltered position. One of the pioneers wrote to an Australian paper as follows:
"I was in the galley getting our evening meal when there came a squall of wind. We were in terror lest the tent should blow away altogether. Tea was forgotten, and we used all our efforts in trying to hold our tent down to the ground. The wind lulled a bit and we went to bed. We got drenched as we lay there, but it was no use turning out. When I got out my pyjamas clung to me as though I had taken a swim in them. Fortunately the rain only lasted that day, and although we had to get into a wet bed the next night, the sun soon shone again."

Another night the single women, who occupied a tent by themselves, were terrified almost out of their wits by a terrifying, long-sustained cry, which they were convinced was that of a tiger lusting for their blood. The animal prowled quite close to their tent, and they expected every moment to be eaten up. For the rest of that night armed men patrolled the camp, and fires were kept burning brightly to scare away savage beasts. In the morning the animal whose awful note had so alarmed the sleepers was found to be a donkey fraternally anxious to greet them. It seems that in parts of Australia that useful animal was little known, so that the ladies did not recognise his welcoming note.

Having had so bitter an experience of Paraguayan rain the colonists turned all their energies at once to the task of building houses. No stone of any description could be found so they were forced to adopt the native mode of construction. Rough hewn corner posts of hard wood were first put in and connected by means of withies and vines. On this light basket structure coat after coat of 'pug' (made by mixing the red clay with water) was daubed. Half a dozen men would be employed in treading the pug, as Eastern people tread the winepress, to mix it well and bring it to the required consistency. Others would lift masses of the pug and throw it against the wicker work. When the whole side was unevenly covered it would be left to harden in the sun and a second dressing applied next day. After the application of several thick coats within and without, the whole was carefully smoothed over and allowed to bake by the heat of the sun into a very substantial wall. Roofs were made either of thatch or of shingles (wooden tiles).

Naturally it was not suggested that these mud huts should serve permanently for human beings to live in. It was intended to utilize them as barns or cowsheds when — in a few months' time — more substantial homes had been put up. As will presently appear, however, the community never had time to spare between its perpetual wrangles to erect civilised buildings, and some of the survivors of the experiment still live in the ruins of the patched and repaired original mud huts to this day.

In the first instance the builders concentrated their attention upon a large hall, 144 ft. by 20 ft., divided into twelve compartments, each to house one family. This building was to be the centre of the township, which was already being laid out in quarter acre allotments, each with a frontage of 66 ft. and a depth of 165 ft. Those in authority strained every nerve to erect a weather-proof house as soon as possible, to prevent the colony's possessions from spoiling, and to receive the Government officers in state when they came to pay an official visit to the new colony.

New Australia Settlement, 1905

CHAPTER VIII.

EARLY DAYS AT NEW AUSTRALIA.

A FEW days after the arrival of the Socialists the Official Gazette in Asuncion published a notice constituting New Australia as a separate district, not subject to the control of the local magistrates at Ajos or at San Jose. In order that they might have proper control over their land the colonists were allowed to nominate three of their members to hold official positions. To the principal office of Administrator (executive officer for enforcing law and registering births, deaths, and marriages) William Lane was appointed, with Tozer as deputy magistrate. Many of the Socialists had the strongest objection to the elevation of three of their number to positions of authority over the rest, but they submitted to the arrangement when told that it was the only way they could guard against outside interference. Gradually they hoped to educate the Government to an appreciation of the blessings of absolute equality. A date, October 7th, was assigned for the official opening of New Australia.

When the day came for the colony's formal recognition the large hall was still unfinished; in fact it was only partially thatched. A tarpaulin was thrown over the unfinished end of the place, a table was knocked together out of boxes, and a thirty foot flag pole was erected to receive the tricoloured flag of Paraguay. Walker had been appointed to conduct the important Government officials to the colony. The party consisted of Dr. Lopez, Minister for Foreign Affairs, the Secretary to the President, and other notables, escorted by a military officer with four soldiers.

After breakfast, then, on the morning of the 7th October, the sounding of a horn proclaimed that the Government party was at hand. The little cavalcade advanced at the trot and halted, without dismounting, till Lane came forward to receive them. Then the Minister and his suite were conducted into the hall, while the soldiers tethered their horses in the orange grove. Dr. Lopez, a good-humoured man, about thirty-eight years of age, with a round, red face, might have been taken for an English squire. When he had accepted what refreshments the colonists could offer the horn sounded again for all to assemble.

After the trustees and committee, consisting of the foreman of each department, had been introduced to the Minister he read a proclamation, which the President's secretary interpreted. The soldiers were drawn up and the Minister unfolded a Paraguayan flag. Each soldier took a corner and thus carried it fifty yards, the party following. Then, facing about, the officer took the flag, the Minister and Mr. Lane linked arms and advanced to the flagstaff, the party following them. The halyards were looped on, and the two hauled together. As the flag with its stripes of red, white and blue, its lion, and its cap of liberty, fluttered in the breeze the colonists cheered and the soldiers fired their Winchesters. Second and third salutes were fired, and the enthusiastic Australians (or Utopians as they might now more properly style themselves) cheered themselves hoarse, standing bareheaded beneath the flag which was to guarantee them their 'emancipation' from all the ills of the British yoke.

The day of its official recognition was one of high festivity at New Australia, and an honest effort was made by all the colonists to compose their differences and join hands heartily in friendship for the sake of the common cause. Something of the old high spirit of hope was revived and there were not wanting those who prophesied that, on a day not far distant, Socialist rule would have spread from their small community to embrace the entire country. It seemed far from improbable that the thousands of Anglo-Saxons who might shortly be expected to join them would become the masters of Paraguay. Not that the New Australians dreamed of abusing the hospitality of the Paraguayans by going to war with them; the country having already a democratic constitution would be converted to Socialism, if at all, by 'peaceful penetration,' and there would be no need to alter so much as the nation's flag, for on that emblem were inscribed the noble words "Paz y Justicia," Peace and Justice.

The refugees from industrial strife, from 'victimisation' and all the alleged horrors of Capitalism felt that the trials they had endured would not have been suffered in vain if peace were found, and justice ruled, at New Australia. But would they do so?

Until sufficient rough housing accommodation had been put up to shelter the whole party from the weather there was little room for bickering, since all were fully employed from daylight till dark upon the work of procuring and preparing the necessary materials. As soon as a few could be spared from such work preparations were made for receiving 2500 head of cattle upon the splendidly situated camp at Las Ovejas, where a great ring fence was required to prevent them from straying. While engaged upon such work the colonists had to contend with numerous difficulties incidental to first settlement in any tropical country. The great clusters of long thorns which tore their clothes to pieces, and other unpleasant features of work in the densely tangled forest made timber getting a painful process. They were unaccustomed to such a pest as the Chigre a small flea which gets under the toenails and lays its eggs, causing the feet to fester. Hornets built their nests under the rafters, and could only be taken down in wet weather, when it was easy to put a lighted rag on the end of a cane and burn them out, though the person performing the operation was pretty sure to be stung. Travelling ants also made periodic visits to each house, driving the occupants out but these were something of a blessing in disguise, for they drove away all other pests, such as cockroaches, spiders, lizards, etc. Parrots, monkeys, and vultures are plentiful also in Paraguay, but they are unobjectionable, except when the former damage the crops, or the latter pick out the eyes of a sickly calf.

At first there was some dread of meeting jaguars, pumas, and ocelots in the forest but these retreated further into the wilderness at once and gave little trouble. Snakes, however, were an ever present danger. As an example of the alarming experiences which befell the colonists may be instanced an adventure of the Jacobsen family. Riding through the high grass towards the house of a neighbour, Jacobsen was alarmed to see his little boy racing towards him along the track, screaming with pain and fright. Hurrying up, he found that a venomous snake had its fangs firmly imbedded in the youngster's calf. With no remedy for snake bite at hand the father did what was best, under the circumstances, in securing a tight bandage above the wound to stop the circulation of the blood. Then he set off on a ride of thirty-five miles to Villa Rica, riding through the night with his boy before him. The roads were very bad at the time and there was great delay on the way. In consequence, though Dr. Botrill, who was a kind friend to the colonists, saved the little boys life, he could not undo the injury the limb had sustained from the tight ligature, and he is lame still.

Mosquitoes also gave great trouble, as the annoying adventure which befell M illustrates. This individual, a real Australian bushman, self-educated (on the most original principles), argumentative, and determined, and a convinced Anarchist, met with a situation out of which even his rugged eloquence could not extricate him. He was riding to Villa Rica on official business one morning, when the burning sun caused infinite discomfort to the most hardened, and was not sorry to reach the shade of the trees on the banks of the Rio Tebicuari. As often happened, the ferryman was absent from his post, and it was necessary to swim the stream. As he was wearing his 'Sunday-best' garments, M undressed and packed them carefully into the waterproof bag secured to his saddle. Then he led his horse into the water. Pondering deeply, as was his habit, over the problems of the Universe, M failed to observe a snag and tripped over it, releasing the horse and floundering wildly in the water. When he regained his feet, the horse had already crossed and was watching him from the opposite side.

Swimming over, M expected to catch his mount without any difficulty, but the animal, which was quite used to being caught by a respectable individual wearing clothes, was not at all willing to surrender to this naked man. M called but the horse edged away and finally kicked up its heels and retired to a safe distance, turning to stare at its angry master with reproachful eyes. After stalking the horse for some time without any success M realised the hopelessness of his position and upbraided the animal in vigorous Australian. In consequence the horse refused to stay longer in his society and galloped away towards Oveido. After its vanishing form M called opprobrious epithets for some time but, before he had half done justice to the situation, a voracious mosquito called his attention to the pressing problem of self-protection. At first he entertained the idea of walking across the camp to some native casa where he could borrow clothes and a horse, but he had forgotten the heat of the sun, which would flay him in half an hour, and he had also left the 'bichos' (insects) out of the reckoning. He was forced to seek shelter in the river to escape the mosquito bites and heat; there, standing with the water up to his chin, in no enviable frame of mind, he waited patiently for some other traveller to arrive and put an end to the ridiculous situation. But hour after hour passed and no one came. At the best of times there is not much traffic across the Tebicuari at that ford, and on this particular day M's evil star provided that no one should come to his assistance.

Through the whole of the day the unfortunate Anarchist remained in the water with a halo of mosquitoes round his head. At nightfall, when he could venture out without being blistered by the sun, he sallied forth and the mosquitoes, their appetites reinforced by their long wait, went with him. Eventually he reached a native hut and was hospitably entertained, clothed, and fed. An hour later he found his horse unconcernedly nibbling the grass at a little distance; it says much for his philosophic spirit that he forbore to visit upon the brute suffering equal to that which the mosquitoes had inflicted upon him.

Such trials as these were as nothing, however, to the acrimonious disputes which once more broke out upon the colony within a few weeks of its official opening.

To take a few minor instances first. An eminent educationalist, Mr. Murdoch, who held an important appointment in Japan, joined the colonists, not as a member but to assist them during the first few months in organising education, and to see how the experiment developed. But he could get no scholars. "Because there were no jams and pickles in the store," Mrs. William Lane told an interviewer after her return to Australia, "the mothers refused to send their children to him. On the other hand a lady and her daughter, who had been appointed to the educational staff of the colony ignoring the settlers' claims, rushed off to the native huts, and there amused themselves in an attempt to teach the Indian children English." The leader's wife also told her Australian friends that three men who had brought saddles (presumably expecting to be appointed stockmen) refused to lend them to the official stockmen, so that the latter had to gallop in pursuit of cattle on make-shift saddles without stirrups! Similarly a colonist who had brought a magic-lantern with him refused to give his brother Socialists an entertainment, though he would exhibit it for the amusement of the natives as often as requested.

The problem of the due apportionment of labour which had threatened a storm upon the Royal Tar, now began to occasion acute controversy. It was freely alleged by almost every colonist against some other that the latter was working less vigorously for the benefit of all than he would have done in his own interest.

Before proceeding to relate what actually occurred at New Australia, it is interesting to note what Socialist theorists claim would be the result of removing from industry the incentive of personal gain.

"I will confess I find it hard to write with any patience and civility of this argument that humanity will not work except for greed or need of money and only in proportion to the getting," says Mr. H. G. Wells. "The public services of the coming civilisation," he insists in the same work, "will demand and will develop a far completer discipline and tradition of honour."

Mr. Robert Blatchford, in the fifteenth chapter of 'Merrie England' sets out to answer the objection:

"Socialism is impossible, because it would destroy the incentive of gain." With his usual dexterity the author plays round and about his theme so cleverly that the uncritical reader may well believe that he has disposed of it, although as a matter of fact, the main issue is completely side-tracked. "It seems an amazing thing to me, this persistence in the belief that greed is the motive power of humanity," he asserts. "The refutation of that error is forever under our noses. You see how men strive at cricket; you see the intense effort and the fierce zeal they display at football; . . . Your volunteer force— does that exist for gain? What will not a soldier do for a tiny bronze cross not worth a crown piece? What will a husband endure for his wife's sake? A father for his children? A fanatic for his religion? But you do not believe that Socialism is to destroy all love, and all honour, and all duty and devotion, do you?"

It seems hardly necessary to remind the intelligent reader that the same man who will try hard to win a football match for fun, or gain the V.C. for glory, without hope of monetary reward, would have the most rooted objection to doing anything so dull as ploughing or brick-laying without due and sufficient recompense. But the optimistic views of 'Nunquam' — who believes that only Socialists understand human nature — were shared by William Lane, who, before his bitter disillusionment, wrote:
"But New Australia won't work , critics say. Why not? Do we labour for gold, think you? Why, no man who is a man would trade the kiss of a woman, or the hand-clasp of a friend, or the arm-clinging of a little child, for the wealth of a Tyson. Give the average man a cottage home, the woman he loves, children in whose eyes his own life laughs back at him, friends who esteem him, food for mind as well as for body, and then see if he will not toil to fence his home from all ill. And he won't toil the less because the fence he works at is a ring fence, which guards his

mates' home as it guards his, when he understands that by co-operation he can make it higher, and stronger, and thicker, than any fence he could possibly put up round his own small yard."

Apparently all the foregoing representative writers think, with Herr August Bebel, that Socialism would revolutionise human nature:

"It is evident that labour thus organised on principles of perfect freedom and democratic equality, in which one represents all, and all one, must awake the highest sense of solidarity and a spirit of cheerful activity, and call forth a degree of emulation such as is nowhere to be found in the present industrial system."

How very delightful it must be to have such beautiful faith in the noble qualities of all one's fellow men. It is upon this conviction that every man is at heart 'sans peur et sans reproche' that Socialists build their hopes of universal bliss. But, as Mr. Blatchford says, "the only school for the study of human nature is the world." The example of New Australia affords a priceless opportunity to study and compare Socialism in practice and in theory. If he had only found time to spend a month or two there, Herr Bebel himself must have admitted the fundamental error of his proposition, for dissension, gloom, and sloth were the order of the day.

In those early days the colonists were intoxicated with the magnificence of their project. There was no steady effort leading up to bigger things. Confident, and with some capital behind them, they commenced at once on the scale they hoped to be able to continue, and one of the first things they decided on was ample leisure. They had done with the bad old scheme of things in which the exigencies of Capitalism ground the people down, robbed them of rest, of energy, of health, of food, of time — so that they have neither heart nor mind nor opportunity to become aught but drudges. At all risks some of the New Australians were determined to avoid drudgery in their new life; they were very keen on being properly 'uplifted'. There was a brass band of thirty-six instruments in the colony, which had cost £25o. "What is the use of a piano, if you have neither leisure nor means to learn to play it?" Mr. Blatchford inquires; like good Socialists the bandsmen practiced on their instruments assiduously in Colony time. On strict Trade Union principles none worked more than eight hours a day, and it was natural that the bandsmen should prefer blowing away at their instruments for some considerable proportion of their time to felling trees in the forest, or tilling the fields beneath the burning rays of a tropical sun. To any practical- minded person who suggested that music might be dispensed with for the present, the musicians could retort, "I tell you, my practical friend, that you ought to have, and may have good music."

A great deal of dissatisfaction was occasioned by the way labour was distributed. The man who worked arduously for eight hours in the vegetable garden envied the more fortunate fellow who spent his day riding about the camp, herding cattle. The cowboy, on the other hand, considered that the schoolmaster had a considerably easier job, and he was perhaps moved to compare his allotted task with that of the colonist whose principal duty appeared to be to blow the dinner horn.

Although there were nominally foremen in charge of different departments, the rank and file regarded it as an intolerable insult to be 'speeded up.' If it were true that under Capitalism "each worker was robbed of two-thirds of all he earned" surely the individual need only work one-third as hard under Socialism to produce an equal result. Moreover, "You often hear industry praised as a virtue, I think the thing is not a virtue in itself ..."

says the most popular text-book of Socialism, "You must not fall into the error of the economist and suppose that the people who produce most are the greatest of the worthiest people. Before praising a nation for its productiveness and industry we should enquire if the things they produce are noble or worthless things, and if the labour of their hands is the labour of slaves — or of freemen. While disentangling the knotty question as to whether the tree one is hewing down, is a noble or a worthless tree, it is just as well for a good Socialist to sit down and have a smoke to assist his cogitations. If a foreman should happen along unheard, and make rude remarks about his apparent idleness, it is the free Socialist's instant duty to retort as forcibly as possible that one is not a slave. If the Socialist has his 'Merrie England' by heart and has presence of mind to quote that 'universal industry, and thrift, and temperance amongst the poor would tend to make them poorer than they now are,' the foreman will retire completely worsted!"

When William Lane initiated his great venture he was a convinced believer in the theory that, once removed from the pernicious influence of Capitalism, they would all dwell together in brotherly love without the necessity for severe restrictions. He soon found out his mistake, however, for bitter charges of favouritism were continually levelled at his head and at the heads of the foremen in charge of every industry. When he found that envy, hatred, and all uncharitableness thrived in this Paradise as in a hot-bed. He decided on a policy of benevolent despotism, which the fact of his holding proxies for all the members of the Association still in Australia enabled him to carry out. With a stern hand he put down revolt, and punished those who disputed his decisions by setting them the most distasteful tasks. No one was allowed to absent himself from the colony without Lane's permission (seldom accorded lest they should be tempted to get drink) and incessant grumbling became the order of the day. It is interesting to compare Mr. Blatchford's statement: "I deny that Socialism would result in any form of slavery at all," with the following extract from a letter written by one of the disillusioned pioneers:

"We have surrendered all civil rights and become mere cogs in a wheel. No longer active factors in the scheme of civilisation. ... In fact a man is practically a slave. Lane does the thinking and the colonists do the work. Result barbarism."

CHAPTER IX.

THE FIRST EXPULSIONS.

Few, even among Socialists, realise the ferocity of Socialism. Of course they are aware of the frightful episodes which occurred during the Reign of Terror in Paris — but they believe that those sanguinary occurrences were occasioned by other contemporary causes, and would not necessarily recur if State Socialism were now established. The few logical Socialists of to-day fully recognise, however, that a period of absolute tyranny — during which all opponents of Socialism, and even all Socialists who failed to agree with the precise views of their brother Socialists in power, would be pitilessly sacrificed for the sake of producing uniformity of aim among its citizens — would usher in the ' Coming State.'

Principally through the influence of the Christian religion modern civilisation is tolerant even towards the unworthy; even the 'won't-work' is accommodated with a bed and a meal in the casual ward; even the useless drunkard is 'given another chance,' and then another, and another, and the worst thing that can happen to him is a period of detention in a gaol; as for the agitator, whose aim in life is to upset the existing scheme of civilisation, he is actually protected by the police force of that civilisation from the natural indignation of other citizens.

Socialism is much too logical to tolerate such a state of affairs. In a small community, expulsion; in an international Socialist State, the lethal chamber, will be the fate of persistent offenders against the established conventions. And this though the executive authorities of the State may be, personally, the mildest and most humane of men. The ferocity of the Socialist State will be, of course, a legalised ferocity; that is, it will be exercised nominally for the benefit of the State. The method of its working will be as emotionless and merciless as the vengeance of the worker bees upon the drones. The officials of the efficient and well-organised Socialist community will not tolerate the presence of drunken, lazy, or trouble-creating citizens in their midst ; Socialism will be no wit less pitiless than the spirit of the hive, when as Maeterlinck records: "one morning the long-expected word of command goes through the hive, and the peaceful workers turn into judges and executioners . . . each one is assailed by three or four envoys of justice . . . and in a very brief space, their appearance becomes so deplorable, that pity, never far from justice in the depths of our hearts, quickly returns, and would seek forgiveness, though vainly of the stern workers who recognise only Nature's harsh and profound laws. Many will reach the door and escape into space . . . but, towards evening, impelled by hunger and cold, they return in crowds to the entrance of the hive to beg for shelter. But there they encounter another pitiless guard. The next morning, before setting forth on their journey, the workers will clear the threshold, strewn with the corpses of the useless giants."

The present writer would be the last to deny that such a system has its merits when applied by a brute Republic with no lesser means of self-protection against brute intelligence incapable of reformation. In a human Republic, however, were such drastic discipline permitted, not merely the drones, but also the most energetic individuals whose views or persons happened to be considered objectionable by the executive would be suppressed. As will presently appear, at New Australia a sentence of banishment was enforced for an offence which a 'Capitalistic' judge would have punished by a fine of ten shillings and costs, plus, perhaps the doctor's fee, at most.

There was considerable friction at New Australia over the total abstinence pledge. To Lane it was no deprivation to go without alcohol, as he was a life-long abstainer, but with others the case was different. After a hard day's work in the forest many men felt that they would be all the better for a tot of the excellent rum made by the natives in the vicinity. Where did the freedom of New Australia come in, when as the Clarion scornfully said of Sicily, "the workers were as temperate as dogs; and they were treated like dogs."

Some argued very reasonably that there was no essential connection between Socialism and Rechabite principles — the wise Dr. Hertzka provided a brewery in Freeland as a matter of course — and requested that the temporary ban on alcohol should be removed. When Lane obstinately refused to give permission some of the colonies decided to dispense with it, for, after all, "is not disobedience, the rarest and most courageous of the virtues?[vi]"

It is characteristic of many stalwart Britishers that, when they are very miserable they find comfort in a glass. Three of the depressed New Australians, visiting a neighbouring native village, revived their flagging spirits wonderfully by a liberal potation, and, on their return, were heartily congratulated by their less courageous mates. But they incurred the fierce wrath of their master. To the consternation of the culprits and their friends Lane decreed their instant expulsion from the community.

Apart from the question of abstract justice this action was so unlike William Lane's previous professions that his followers were absolutely staggered. They might have quoted Mr.

Blatchford;
"Drunkenness is a disease. It is just as much a disease as typhus fever or cholera, and often arises from very similar causes. Any medical man will tell you that the craving for alcoholic stimulants is frequently found amongst men whose nervous system is low."

Surely the New Australians had had enough to try their nerves? They might have reminded him that in the old days, when he preached brotherly love and mutual forbearance in the columns of The Worker he wrote thus of a Shearers' Union organiser, who, it was alleged, had embezzled certain money belong-ing to his mates: "I deeply regret that the committee of the A.L.U. have decided to prosecute. I deny he is a criminal. He is a poor drunken wretch who should have been safeguarded against himself."

How was it possible to harmonise so merciful a spirit with his present determination? The answer is simple. Although it rails so bitterly against the despotism of all existing authority Socialism is necessarily infinitely more despotic in enforcing its own counsels of perfection. That is why all attempts at Socialistic government inevitably prove the most hateful form of grinding tyranny. As the faithful servant of the 'Cause' Lane was compelled, in spite of any regrets he might personally feel, to deal pitilessly with offenders.

It would have been easy for Lane to punish the three culprits by docking their credit at the store, and many of the settlers begged him to adopt that course, but Lane was obdurate. They had broken his pet regulation, and they must go. In vain it was pointed out that an article of the Constitution said, "Dismissal from the community for persistent or unpardonable offence against the well-being of the community to be decreed only by a five-sixth majority of all adult members." He replied that the Constitution was not yet in operation and that if it were, his sole vote (representing all those still in Australia) outweighed the others by the required majority. The fact that the unfortunate offenders would be stranded in an Indian country many thousands of miles from home did not move him, nor did the fact that they had contributed all their possessions to his wildcat scheme. There was neither room in New Australia for backsliders, nor mercy for them.

In the masterful manner in which he now conducted affairs, Lane issued the following decree :

NOTICE
All members will take notice that 'L' and 'W' have been expelled from the New Australia Co-operative Association for wilful and persistent violation of the clause in our mutual agreement, signed by them, relating to liquor drinking.
Dec. 15th, 1893. W. Lane.
(Chairman.)

An uproar followed the posting of this notice, for it was claimed that others besides the three men mentioned were guilty of obtaining liquor. In fact certain of Lane's best friends were accused of being persistent sinners, and the allegation that personal animus had existed in Australia between one of the expelled and one of Lane's most trusted henchmen was adduced as evidence of victimisation. On these and other grounds feeling ran high and it was asked if the three offenders declined, as they did decline, to go; how could their expulsion be enforced when half the colony sided with them?

Socialist agitators are fond of declaiming against the use, by the authorities, of military power to overawe mutinous mobs who refuse to obey the law. If they were asked how a Socialist executive would deal with a case such as that which arose at New Australia — where a large proportion of the citizens on the spot upheld the law-breakers — it would puzzle them to provide an answer. The fact is that nine out of ten Socialists believe that no police would be required in a Socialist State. Yet Trade Union tyranny might warn them that a Socialist Government would enforce its will upon the rank and file by shot and steel if necessary. This fact is frankly admitted by the greatest intellect in the Socialist ranks to-day. Bernard Shaw, 'The Revolutionists' Handbook':

"Of course, if the nation adopted the Fabian policy it would be carried out by brute force exactly as our present property system is. It would become the law; and those who resisted it would be fined, sold up, knocked on the head by policemen, thrown into prison, and in the last resort 'executed' just as when they break the present law."

William Lane was too clever a man to issue decrees which he had no power of enforcing. His appointment from the Paraguayan Government, as executive officer for enforcing law, gave him the power to call upon that Government for force to back up his decisions. On the expelled members refusing to quit, he disappeared from the colony, and returned later with a body of Paraguayan soldiers armed to the teeth. Holding with Mr. Blatchford that "in a Socialistic state of society they would no more go armed and in fear of their fellow creatures," the colonists had sold any weapons they might possess for the benefit of the common fund; they had no better weapons than agricultural implements and sticks to oppose to Lane's revolver and the murderous looking bayonets of his native posse. In vain the 'expelled begged for mercy, in vain they demanded the return in full of their contributions (one of the expelled had contributed £1,000 to the common funds) — but these were a 'voluntary gift' to the Association — in vain women wept and declared that they and their families would secede also if the three unfortunates were so heavily punished for so light a crime. Although it was the festive Christmas season Lane was adamant.

One of the colonists, described as 'neither a seceder nor one of the Lane's puppets' wrote the following account of the expulsion to the Barrier Miner:
"Upon the day appointed for them to leave, the police came down upon the scene. There did really appear to be a serious prospect of blood-shed. Lane rode in and about with a revolver in his belt. It was not as though the men who had to leave were an entirely bad lot. Only one was very bad. Two or three others only were not good, but amongst the rest were some really first class workers, and some of the women, too, could ill be Spared. They left peaceably however, and I do not know who were the most miserable — those who went (the expelled by the way were joined by some voluntary seceders) or those of us who remained, and we have been pretty miserable ever since..."

He continues:
"...We had Christmas dinner all together, and I can't say we were happy. It was just after the trouble. For the youngsters the women folk managed to rake up some cards and so on to make quite a presentable Christmas tree. Santa Claus, however, did not seem to get as far as Paraguay. . . ."

There was of course no religious service at New Australia on Christmas Day, but the party were assembled to sing the marching song of their movement:

Shoulder to shoulder, mates,

Shoulders together,
Hands clasped in hands my mates,
Fair and fine weather,
Hearts beating close, my mates,
Each man a brother,
Building a home, my mates,
All for each other.

The children sang heartily enough, but the men listened for the most part in gloomy silence. They were thinking of their 'mates' who had just been shouldered out, with scarcely enough money to enable them to reach Asuncion and throw themselves upon the mercy of the British Consul. Lane's utterances upon the subject of mateship woke little response now in the hearts of those who remained. Was it mateship to induce a man to contribute all he had in the world to the 'Cause,' and then expel him with only three pounds in his pocket? Was it to do such things as this that they had left Australia?

CHAPTER X.

A HELL UPON EARTH.

The men and women who had left happy homes in a civilised country to teach the world a glorious lesson were sadly undeceived at New Australia. Lane's strict insistence upon the letter of the law, the suspension of the Constitution (of which the rank and file were not aware till they had sailed), and the expulsion of members caused the bitterest animosity amongst the colonists. In fear and trembling men and women assembled in groups to discuss the crisis in their affairs with bated breath. Practically no work was done, the days and nights being spent by rival factions in intriguing one against the other. Finally the disaffection became so acute that about one-third of the party decided to take concerted action; how eagerly now they turned towards the British flag which they had repudiated so cheerfully a little earlier. An authentic account of what actually occurred is to be found in the Foreign Office Report, 'Miscellaneous Series,' No. 358 (1895), which reads as follows :

"Things went from bad to worse, disputes arose and became so bitter that two parties were formed, one composed of those who followed and the other of those who opposed the directions of the manager, and a new source of quarrel sprang up when it was discovered that the Association had been registered as a limited liability company, without the members having ever been consulted on the subject, and that the manager would be able to exercise almost absolute power; moreover the use of the police force created great excitement and a general uproar, until at length finding it impossible to agree eighty-five members seceded in a body, preferring to abandon all their shares in the colony and to receive a certain sum, the married about 200 dollars and the single 150 dollars.

"In a letter which one of the seceders wrote to the British Consul at Monte Video he stated that the manager had arrogated to himself absolute power, and was expelling those who dared to stand up for their rights by twos and threes. 'To prevent his taking us thus,' so he says, 'we have all decided to leave in the hope that something may be done for us in a body that would not be done for us individually.'

"They went to Villa Rica, and there they had a long list of grievances to pour forth, and tales to tell of how some had been expelled on trivial pretexts and others tyrannised. They said that no financial statement had ever appeared, that when they had asked for one they had been terrorised, that they could not go outside the settlement without leave; It was, of course, necessary to register the Association in Paraguay, as a land company in order to secure its legal status. It was expressly stipulated that the shares should pay no dividend, that if they did attempt to go, having given up everything they possessed for the good of the cause, they had no money to spend. Life under such conditions was intolerable, and it was clear that what with the absence of liberty, the isolation of existence, the suspicion with which one party regarded the other, the mutual fear, the boycotting, the constant disputes, the hundreds of little disagreeable events that went on the whole day long, whatever opinions they might hold on other subjects they were one and all disposed to agree that New Australia was anything but a working man's paradise."

Naturally the British Consul at Asuncion was at his wits' end to know what to do with this army of destitute fellow countrymen, and the Second Secretary of the Legation at Buenos Aires was sent to try and patch up a truce.

"I had been instructed to visit the Colony to enquire into the cause of the expulsion of these members and the secession of about one-third of the colony," wrote Mr, M. de C. Findlay, "They were given a few pounds apiece when they left, but when I saw them they were on the verge of destitution.
"I found Mr. Lane, the present chairman of the Association, prepared to give me all the information I asked for, but to him the Articles of Association and agreements signed are as the code of the Medes and Persians, and any infringement thereof must be summarily dealt with. He does not admit such things as extenuating circumstances, justice means to him the law according to the letter; a man is either 'straight' or he is not straight and in the latter case he should go. . . . Another question which may cause differences is that of nationality. Mr. Lane told me he had no reason to be enthusiastically loyal and that a vote would be taken before long which would probably result in the adoption of a Paraguayan nationality"

In his introductory letter Mr. Findlay testifies to the good character of the Utopians:
"The colonists have started with everything in their favour — free land, immunity from taxation, a good climate, and a certain amount of capital. They are a fine class of men, and if they were less disposed to stand on the letter of their rights and took a more reasonable view of the failings of their fellows they would be sure to succeed. As it is they came to found Utopia, and before I visited the colony had succeeded in creating (as they said) 'a hell upon earth.' I feel morally certain that if the colony had been started on an individualistic basis (each colonist receiving an allotment), and with no complicated regulations to fight over, not a man would have left the settlement."

Mr. Findlay found it impossible to patch up a truce between Lane and the seceders, who must have starved but for the generosity of the Paraguayan Government which housed and fed them for three weeks at Villa Rica, while they were debating what was best to be done. When he learned that the negotiations had failed President Gonzalez offered the seceders (but not the three expelled members) a grant of land, on individualistic lines, at the Gonzalez Colony, which he had established two years before quite near the railway line. With indefatigable zeal Mr. Findlay set out to this place where he found Frenchmen, Germans, and Poles doing well. The President offered to provide each family with thirty acres of land, which would be increased if they showed industry, together with agricultural implements and tools, a cow and a calf, and a yoke of oxen, all at cost price (to be paid for on easy terms spread over a number of years). Furthermore, seeds were to be provided free, and colonists would be exempt from taxation for ten years. In addition the settlers were offered a weekly sustenance allowance for the first six months be spent at a Government store where meat would be sold at cost price. With the exception of a few who had obtained employment at Asuncion, the seceders gladly availed themselves of this offer and were conveyed to the Gonzalez (afterwards re-christened 'National') Colony at the Government's expense.

It would be pleasant to be able to record that these unhappy people prospered in their new surroundings, but unfortunately that was not so. The Paraguayan Revolution of July, 1894, drove President Gonzalez from ofiice, and, in the confusion which followed, his generous arrangements for the seceders' benefits were suspended. As they had not yet had time to grow crops on the clearings they had made in the forest the seceders came perilously near to starvation, and, in September, twenty-five of them realised all their resources and took boat to Buenos Aires. Landing penniless in the Argentine capital, they were befriended by the Benevolent Society, which made an appeal to the British charities to aid in returning them to Australia.

When news of their good fortune reached the struggling sixty who still remained at Gonzalez Colony, they jumped to the conclusion that the British Government was anxious to re-patriate them, and one of their number was despatched to Asuncion to interview the Consul on the subject.

"On being told that no such instructions had been received, he said that he would bring his wife and four children and leave them at the door of the Consulate, that his railway fare had been raised by subscription, and he invited Her Majesty's Consul to come and see the miserable plight in which they were."

It is hard to say what would have become of these ruined and desperate folk if the country they had scorned and left had not taken pity on them. On hearing of their sad condition the Australian Government made arrangements to bring them home to start life again in the land where many of them had once been fairly prosperous. Reported Mr. Peel of the Buenos Aires Legation:

"One little band, as they came down the Parana, passed a ship flying the British flag, and forgetting for the moment all their trouble, their losses, their keen disappointment and their destitute condition, broke into a cheer. It was the first time they had seen a British flag since their arrival in Paraguay, and its sight recalled the homes, the friends, and the life-long associations they had so rashly left, and to which they were so anxious to return, and bitterly did they recollect how . . . they had been told by those who had induced them to leave Australia that they had so little cause to be enthusiastically loyal."

Meanwhile organisation was proceeding briskly in Australia, and the return of the Royal Tar on December 7th, 1893, gave a sharp fillip to recruiting. Those aboard of her gave such a good account of the safe and pleasant voyage that the second contingent — already encamped under canvas — was anxious to be gone. Among members of, the Association in the Adelaide district there was quite a rush to sell up their homes, in order to pay in the minimum contribution before the next boat sailed.

It happened that three prominent strike leaders were just then released from prison; when they announced their intention of shaking the dust of Australia from their feet a profound sensation was created in Trade Union circles. A great crowd of sympathisers saw them off by the S.S. Buninyong, which carried ninety-four men, two women, and six children to Monte Video. Burning speeches moved all who were present at the send-off to a great envy of those who were bound for the land of freedom.

"We only wish we were going with you," declared many who had not yet managed to scrape together the necessary sixty pounds. "Look out for us on the other side!"'

In most of the Australian States organisation proceeded so rapidly that the authorities were very much alarmed. If merely the ne'er-do-wells of the community had been joining there would have been no occasion to worry; but the organisers took care to accept only the best material. The Association was said to be negotiating for the purchase of three more ships, and there was no reason to doubt the estimate that, within six years, 6,000 souls would leave for Paraguay. Could nothing be done to stop the wholesale departure of Australia's sturdiest sons? How could the country's broken finances be restored to a healthy condition if all the best brawn and sinew were withdrawn?

If only the true state of affairs at New Australia had been known there would have been no cause for anxiety. But not a hint of the dissension had leaked out when the next batch boarded the Royal Tar at Adelaide on December 28th, 1893. Utterly unsuspicious of the misery their friends were already enduring, the families in this contingent played at 'liberty, equality, and fraternity' as gaily as the Royal Tar's earlier passengers had done. But just as the boat was upon the eve of sailing the emigrants' friends on shore were startled by the publication of the following announcement :
"The Lieutenant Governor has received a telegram from the Secretary of State for the Colonies, informing him that the British Minister at Buenos Aires has telegraphed him to the effect that the British Consul in Paraguay wires that eight New Australians have left their new labour colony as a protest against injustice of administration. They ask that their friends at Adelaide be advised so as to prevent further shipments in Royal Tar, which sails in a few days."

It will be observed that, through some error in transmission, the number of seceders was given as eight instead of eighty. But for this unfortunate blunder the sequel would certainly have been different.

Immediately on receiving this message the Premier made an effort to save the party which had just embarked from the misery in store for them. Detective Segerland was sent out to the boat with the Governor's cable, and with instructions to say that any who wished to leave were still at liberty to do so. It is only just to state that the organisers gave the authorities every facility. When Segerland reached the Royal Tar, Mr. Casey, who was in charge, at once called a meeting for the detective to address, and himself proposed a hearty vote of thanks to the authorities for placing the matter before them. Afterwards a discussion took place, and all agreed that so small a number of secessions as eight was not of any importance. It was if anything a tribute to the courage and rectitude of the administration. A resolution was proposed expressing the greatest confidence in the officials at New Australia and carried unanimously. The proceedings ended with three hearty cheers for William Lane, the detective was sent ashore, and without further ado the Royal Tar was towed out to sea. She sailed without a soul on board having the least suspicion of the deplorable state of affairs at New Australia.

CHAPTER XL.

WILLIAM LANE SECEDES.

On reaching Monte Video and hearing a full report of the dismissals and secessions from New Australia three or four families, to whom it would not mean absolute ruin decided to turn back and take up their old occupations. Most however, decided to go on. After the sacrifices they had made and the distance they had come the majority would not be lightly deterred from the effort to realise the hopes which had so far led them on. When the party were met at Asuncion on March 7th, 1894, by William Lane, his magnetic power still swayed them so effectually that doubts were dispelled and next day all save one left for New Australia. The one "had no sooner landed than he went to the Consulate and claimed protection of the British flag. . . . This emigrant stated that he had no desire to go to New Australia, as he wished to avoid getting into serious trouble, which he thought would probably arise... and that as he had a good deal of personal property which, perhaps, according to the articles of the Association, would not be restored to the original owner, he claimed the protection of the British flag to get it back by all peaceful means."

The remainder of the party, consisting of about 190 persons, proceeded to New Australia, where Lane ordered them to encamp at Loma Rogua, a place about ten miles distant from Las Ovejas, the original settlement. This deliberate isolation of the newcomers was, of course, a precautionary measure intended to prevent them from becoming infected with the general discontent. Naturally, however, it was not long before some of the pioneers visited them and the events leading up to

the expulsions and secession were discussed at length. From that
moment it was determined that Lane's autocratic sway must end.

After hearing their mates' accounts of all that had occurred feeling against the leader they had so long revered ran high amongst the newcomers. And yet — calmly considered — what wrong had he committed? If they had not been blinded by prejudice they would have realised that it was not William Lane, but the whole impracticable scheme that was at fault. Of their own volition they had set up a system of cast-iron laws and regulations and put him in supreme authority with a mandate to enforce them. The man to whom they had temporarily entrusted their voting proxies was, without question, as rigidly honourable, and as innocent of self-seeking as any man could be. By putting in operation the harsh law of expulsion against the three offenders he had acted from the loftiest and most logical motives and, strictly speaking, had not exceeded his authority. It was Socialism rather than William Lane that had offended, for even Mr. Blatchford grants "that State Socialism would imply some interference with the liberty of the individual." And if any liberty is to be absolutely curtailed, which could more properly be suppressed than the liberty to get drunk?

The reasonableness of such arguments as the above will appeal to any fair-minded person but it is the special privilege of democracies to be unreasonable. The British coal miners recently threw over their old leaders, when the enforcement of the Eight Hours' Act, for which they had given a mandate, resulted in a diminution of their earnings; in their place they elevated new leaders who promised that in future they should both eat their cake and have it. In precisely the same manner the New Australians, while insisting that their leader should enforce the regulation, determined to sacrifice him as soon as it appeared that some of their number had suffered through his obedience.

The most varied and violent accusations were levelled at Lane's head by those who wished to displace him. The official 'New Australia: A Report presented to the British Board of the New Australia Association' contains an assortment of charges which, whether well founded or not, are decidedly instructive, as they show the state of feeling which had arisen, and the suspicion with which the over-zealous leader was regarded. In this Report, by one in hearty sympathy with the movement, there is an interesting illustration of the magic change which the exercise of his authority can produce in the attitude of the Socialist rank and file towards their chosen leader. Mr. Rogers alleged:

"Lane as a high-souled enthusiast in the cause of Labour, and Lane as a despot . . . were two different men. As the first he roused the enthusiasm of thousands, as the second he was able to draw out all the worst passions and the most evil thoughts of those whom he had so far led. Hence the first split."

It was not to be expected that experienced Trade Union leaders who had gone to prison for vigorous resistance to 'oppression' in the Antipodes, would tamely submit to what they considered worse oppression at New Australia. Soon after the arrival of the second batch there came a crisis. The newcomers insisted on going thoroughly into matters, and declared that the affairs of the settlement had been so woefully mismanaged that a change of officials was urgently necessary.

Owing to the fact that Lane could not be displaced without his own consent (having been accorded the power of director for two years from the Colony's establishment), the majority would have had a difficulty in enforcing their views had he been obdurate. But he bowed to the will of the people, and telegraphed to his associates in Australia for their consent to the immediate putting in force of the democratic form of government set out in the hitherto suspended Constitution (see end of Chapter II). Immediately permission arrived, he resigned his office, and a new Chairman was appointed with more limited powers.

Of course Lane's fall was the signal for a general deposition of his most trusted lieutenants and fore- men, none of whom relished the notion of being reduced to the ranks and disciplined by the very individuals who hated them most. Lane therefore applied to the new management for permission to retire to a part of the concession called Codas, there to found a third village settlement on the same lines as the two at Las Ovejas and Loma Ruga. There upon a furious outcry arose and it was most unfairly alleged that, even before reaching Paraguay, Lane had decided upon separating with a chosen few from the main body, and that he reserved the choicest ground in the concession, Codas, for this purpose.

Although New Australia held 600 square miles of territory, not more than about one-tenth of which had yet been explored, there was no room on it for William Lane, except as an underling. Permission to settle at Codas was refused by the Board of Management. He was at liberty to leave the colony altogether as others had done, or he could settle down to his share of the common toil, and work for the benefit of his fellow-men in whatever capacity the properly elected authorities might order. The tables were turned with a vengeance.

Faced with these alternatives, William Lane chose the former, and went out into the wilderness accompanied by forty-five adult sympathisers and about a dozen children, together with a fair proportion of the implements and a few head of cattle. Leaving his party encamped by the side of a stream just off the New Australia territory, William Lane went moodily to Asuncion and requested a further grant on which to set up a selected Paradise.

The student of history will discern a close similarity between the march of events at New Australia and that classic pattern of Socialist administration — the Reign of Terror. By an interesting coincidence exactly a century elapsed between the two experiments.

Jean Paul Marat, the French Revolutionist, was as educated and refined a man as William Lane, (though without his humane disposition). Like the latter, Marat had lived in several countries and was a successful professional man (he practiced in London and Paris as a doctor). Marat also was bitten with a feverish desire to benefit 'the people.' In 1789 he launched his paper, L'Ami du Peuple and used its columns to urge the reforms he advocated, just as Lane founded The Worker, one hundred years later for the same purpose. Marat's lease of life as the people's idol lasted till 1792, when the Girondists captured the popular fancy and secured his overthrow. Had Jean Paul lived a century later he might have dreamed of leading his partisans from the stricken field, but his activities were cut short by the hand of a woman assassin in the very month during which, one hundred years later, William Lane sailed in the Royal Tar.

When Marat was thrown out, his place in the mob's affections was divided between the Girondist leaders, Brissot, Gensonn, Vergniaud, Ducos, and Sillery. But a few months after they had driven Marat from power, the Girondists were in turn displaced by an extremer party; and the five who had thought themselves secure were guillotined on the night of October 30th, 1793.

Next the Montagnards wielded brief authority, until the notorious Hebert (who set up Reason as the people's only God) hounded them from office and cast some into prison. But his sway endured not long, for Danton and Robespierre combined to drag him down, and Hebert "died amid the jeers of the mob whose passion for blood he had helped to arouse," a fortnight before the very men he had himself condemned. Next it was Danton's turn, for the treacherous Robespierre bade him begone also, and his head dropped into the basket with Desmoulins' on April 5th, 1794.

As a tribute to his willing sacrifice of all his friends to sate their appetite for change, the sovereign people endured Robespierre's reign for three and a half months more before they invoked the aid of Madame Guillotine to eject him from the 'ideal' Commonwealth, — St. Just and Couthon losing their heads with him, on July 8th, 1794.

Any person who dismisses the appalling incidents of the Reign of Terror as the work of homicidal lunatics, or blames the criminal classes for shedding the blood of France's noblest sons, betrays lamentable ignorance of the acknowledged facts. The assassinations and wholesale executions, the merciless slaughter of everyone whose intellectual opinions did not precisely coincide with the standard temporarily in vogue, were planned and ordered, in the name of progress, by mild-mannered, well-meaning philosophers, who were convinced that they were thereby helping on the millennium. Though the ruling majority in a modern Socialist State might be less enamoured of summary executions, it would be no wit more tolerant, and would undoubtedly reduce society to a state of abject slavery, or else of Anarchy.

Every prominent Socialist rejects the suggestion that Socialism means slavery; but how many people realise that Anarchy is the definite goal towards which at least some popular leaders of Socialist thought are consciously striving? Not bomb-throwing Anarchy, of course (though there be some English Socialists who regard even that as a permissible prelude to the establishment of the ideal state), but 'true and noble Anarchism.'

Mr. H. G. Wells states candidly
"That Anarchist world, I admit, is our dream, we do believe — well, I, at any rate, believe this present world, this planet, will some day bear a race beyond our most exalted and temerarious dreams, a race begotten of our wills and the substance of our bodies, a race, so I have said it, 'who will stand upon the earth' as one stands upon a footstool and laugh and reach out their hands amidst the stars, but the way to that is through education and discipline and law. Socialism is the preparation for that higher Anarchism; painfully, laboriously we mean to destroy false ideas of property and self, eliminate unjust laws and poisonous and hateful suggestions and prejudices, create a system of social right-dealing and a tradition of right-feeling and action. Socialism is the schoolroom of a true and noble Anarchism, wherein by training and restraint we shall make free men."

Of course Mr. Wells does not desire the immediate realisation of his dream — the context makes that clear — it is probable that he, personally, anticipates that his 'hot-eared, ill-kempt people' will need a good deal of restraint and law and discipline, spread over a considerable period, before he can let them loose with any feeling of security. But, once converted to his theory of the ideality of Anarchism, will the "hot-eared, ill-kempt people .

. . who," as he says, "are pitiful, and weak, and vain, and touchy, almost beyond measure," be willing to wait till Mr. Wells takes a less pessimistic view of their limitations? Will they not rather in their touchy, hot-eared fashion, call the preacher of discipline and restraint a would-be tyrant, and treat him as the New Australians treated Lane? Will they not impatiently set about the instant 'reform' of the State, as the Girondists, and the Montagnards, and the New Australians set about it; and forthwith set up a by no means noble Anarchism?

In the words of that amazingly candid Socialist, Mr. Bernard Shaw, "If our political ruin is to come, it will be effected by ardent reformers, and supported by enthusiastic patriots as a series of necessary steps in our progress."

Whatever his limitations, William Lane was at least a disinterested leader, inspired by the highest motives, and with a clear and definite idea of the goal towards which he desired to kick the ball of State. His successors were quite as well-meaning, but hardly equally clever, and entirely lacked the personal magnetism which is of such value in a leader. Leaving William Lane for the time being, it will be instructive to follow, for a chapter or two, his successors' adventures in mis-government.

CHAPTER XII.

FREE AND NOBLE ANARCHISM.

After the departure of William Lane from New Australia it was felt that the way was clear for a sane and practical carrying out of the co-operative principle.

Now what is the co-operative principle? How does it work so far as the appointment of officials for instance, is concerned? All this is explained by Laurence Gronlund in 'The Co-operative Commonwealth: An Exposition of Modern Socialism.' The author asserts that in his 'ideal state' "personal responsibility and instant dismissal for failure will permeate the whole service from top to bottom." This will be secured by providing '"first, that all appointments be made from below; next, that the directors stay in office as long as they give satisfaction and not a moment beyond; and, lastly, that all laws and regulations of a general nature must first be ratified by those immediately interested."

These principles were considered wholly admirable by the workers at New Australia. But what about dismissals?

"Every directing official should be given the right instantly to dismiss any one of his subordinates for cause assigned. . . . When, then, a foreman was inefficient, he would be removed instantly, without trial, by his superintendent; he again, might be removed by his bureau-chief — perhaps for abuse of power in removing the foreman; — this bureau-chief again, by his department-chief.

"But the latter official, to whom shall he be responsible? Suppose we make every department chief liable to removal by the whole body of his subordinates. That is to say, suppose that, whenever the workers of a given department inclusive of foremen, superintendents, and other officials, become dissatisfied with their chief, they all meet in their different localities and vote on the dismissal of that chief, and that he be considered removed from office the moment the collective judgment of the whole department is known, if that judgment be adverse to him. Then the bureau-chiefs immediately proceed to elect another chief of department who can be removed in like manner, if he should not suit the workers."

From the point of view of the rank and file there could hardly be devised a better means of ensuring that all officials should be principally concerned to kow-tow to the workers. But what about the latter? — would it be conversant with the dignity of labour for them to be hectored by the very foremen they had themselves elected? By no means!

"Can the foreman also dismiss any of his workers for inefficiency or other causes?" the champions of the rights of man proceeds. "For such cases a trial by his comrades might be provided, the issue of which might be removal to a lower grade or some sort of compulsion. Now is this not Democracy?"

Undoubtedly that is Democracy — of a brand to make the weary labourer rejoice. How such a democratic system works out in practice will presently appear.

Now that the New Australians had liberty to apply their Constitution, they lost no time in examining it with care and with a view to making it truly democratic. Naturally the first step towards this was the alteration of the regulations which gave the least discretionary powers to any individual. In a public meeting assembled, the colonists revised some laws and added many others (see Appendix C), which were in turn revised, and re-revised each time an amateur law-maker could catch the public fancy with any addition or emendation. The unfortunate Secretary had to work overtime in order to keep an accurate record of the sovereign people's ever-changing decisions.

A glance at Appendix C shows that Mr. Blatchford's dictum, "the fact is that under Socialism there would be as few officials, and as many workers, as possible," is not borne out by the history of New Australia. To limit the powers of the Director (or Administrator' as he came to be called) a Board of Management was appointed. This Board was composed of the Director, and a Deputy Director, assisted by two managers from each of the five village settlements now established, who were them-selves elected by the inhabitants of the respective settlements. In addition , each division had its departmental superintendent, etc., whose time was largely taken up in struggling with statistics, which had to be furnished once a week at least to the Deputy Director. Although the total population was only 217, there were, in addition to the officials already enumerated, separate foremen over each of the following departments : — building, forestry, surveying, farming, gardening, stock, dairy, black-smiths, tinsmiths, butchers, bootmakers, culinary, laundry, educational. Any of these, as also the Treasurer, Secretary, etc., were liable to be displaced at any time by a snap-majority against them. As there were always a number of opposition candidates desirous of occupying every official's place, vote canvassing went on continuously and ballots were for a time of almost daily occurrence.

By Rule 30 (see Appendix C) it was provided that "Any twenty-five members may at any time take the initiative and convene a public meeting, of which seven days' notice shall be given, for the consideration of any stated business ; such meeting may select its own chairman, and, provided a two-thirds majority be obtained, at a ballot vote seven clear days after such meeting, the decision arrived at shall be held valid and become law."

The convening of public meetings was found so much more interesting than labour that the new Administrator could hardly sign his name without someone or other insisting on a vote, as to whether it was proper for him to do so. Moreover, the debates gained greatly in liveliness from the fact that some of the women attended regularly, and expressed their views very forcibly, and at any length they pleased, with lofty disregard of the Chairman's ruling. In place of the despotism of one man, the colonists now suffered under the infliction of an inconstant public opinion, which displaced officials, or made new regulations, one day, only to reverse its decisions the next. Under the new regime no subordinate foreman was entrusted with the smallest discretionary power. All applications for clothes, tools, leave of absence, etc., came before the Board of Management, which wasted its time in interminable arguments over petty details, with the result that important matters were hopelessly neglected. Meanwhile organisation in Australia had almost ceased, and no money was coming in from outside; it was therefore vitally necessary for all to co-operate in revenue-producing labour.

Although enormous energy had been expended in the work of clearing the forest, to plant wheat, the crop was unsuitable for the country and had proved a failure. It was therefore necessary to buy corn from the natives, and the little money remaining was expended in this manner. In addition, a debt of two hundred pounds was contracted for the purchase of other articles. Why the pioneers had not already engaged in lumbering operations, or dairy-farming, for profit (they had seventy milk cows, and butter brings a very high price in Villa Rica), to say nothing of cattle dealing, it would be hard to explain. Apparently the directors imagined, as our Socialist legislators do, that they could for ever live on capital. If any questioned the advisability of this or that expenditure, there were always the contributions of future members to look forward to.

By the end of 1894 was confidently anticipated that at least 2000 more would be brought to the colony and it seemed safe enough to count in advance upon their financial offerings to meet any present indebtedness — a line of reasoning identical with that of those municipal administrators who achieve present popularity by cheerfully piling up debts for posterity to pay.

With a view to raising more capital (and to give a much-needed fillip to recruiting) Gilbert Casey was dispatched to Australia with plenary powers, to take over the books, documents, cash, Royal Tar, and other securities, and to place the organisation upon a proper footing. On arrival in Sydney, however, Casey found the officials of the Association not disposed to give him much assistance, since they were strongly on the side of William Lane. Casey quite expected some thousands of pounds worth of assets to be handed over, but in this he was sorely disappointed. When he requested the Australian Secretary to make the necessary transfers he was informed that the Royal Tar was heavily mortgaged, and that no assets could be handed over until certain onerous conditions had been complied with.

The situation was rendered still more awkward by a judgment, delivered in the District Court, in favour of J. H. Smiles (a member of the New Australia Association, who had contributed all he possessed although he had not yet embarked for South America) who claimed the return of the balance of his contribution, over and above the £10 deposit money. As soon as this decision was made known an enormous number of similar claims arose against the Association, and the officials were at their wits' end to know what to do. Casey's own position was particularly embarrassing since his footsteps were dogged by unfortunates, who had paid in their all to the Association and were left stranded in Adelaide or Sydney. Among the most pressing problems demanding his attention was the case of seventeen most respectable women, wives of some of the settlers who left with the first contingent in July, 1893. It had been arranged that the husbands should go first to prepare a home, and that their wives should sail by one of the later boats. In the meantime they were herded together in a four-roomed cottage, penniless, but provided for by orders from the Association's secretary on local tradespeople. As eighteen months had elapsed already, the husbands were naturally indignant with the Association for not dispatching the seventeen stranded women to Paraguay, and Casey had instructions to attend to the matter without delay. When he reached Australia he found, to his horror and dismay, that the tradespeople had long since refused to give them further supplies, and that the bailiffs were ejecting them from the house for non-payment of rent. A woman, whose husband had contributed £400 to the Association, had to depend on charity for a crust to eat at Christmas 1894.

The position of the other stranded folk, who had already passed nearly two years in tents awaiting permission to sail, was serious enough, but the plight of the seventeen women, separated by thousands of miles of ocean from their husbands, was desperate indeed. In their interest Casey took the courageous course of issuing a plain statement to the press, although he knew that this course would produce a plentiful crop of hostile criticism, and add to the difficulties of further organisation. The appeal was addressed to the Unionists, Democrats, Socialists, and members of the New Australia Association, in Queensland:

"I am personally known to a very large number of you. I have done some fairly conscientious work for all of you, and have been paid for the same. Still, I fancy that there is something outside of the mere cash payment that gives me the right to claim your assistance now. I have undertaken the gigantic task of re-organising the New Australia movement and I want your help. I want to deal fairly, squarely, and aboveboard with those I am working for and with. This appeal is issued upon my own responsibility, in order that I may succeed in the task I have undertaken. To do that I must have the assistance of outsiders just now, because our Association has been left absolutely stone broke; because it has a number of unfortunate women and children left on its hands whose husbands and fathers have been in Paraguay for the last twelve months; because it is cruelty to let this continue any longer through the fear of being sneered a by those who misunderstand or have no sympathy with the movement; because many of our members gave up all their possessions to the Association officials, left their employment as instructed, and have been in destitute circumstances ever since; these unfortunates cannot be expected to do a great deal towards assisting others, though they are doing their level best; because there is no hope of the Association getting anything out of the Tar or other property; because it is better to abandon the attempt than fool round with the law; because it is right to send these people across; because £500 will send them all to their husbands and fathers; because finally a small sum from each of our friends will do what is needed, and my trust in men and women is great enough to make me feel absolutely certain that this money will be received before the first week in January."

Casey's intentions were good, but it would really have been kinder on his part to advise the stranded members of the association to beg their bread rather than proceed to New Australia. However, he still had faith in the great scheme, and began to enroll fresh recruits in face of a strong opposition. By this time (January, 1895) one or two of the seceders had contrived to get back to Australia, and did all in their power to dissuade others from sailing. Mr. Pope in the Adelaide Advertiser:
"It makes me sad to hear that they are so misguided as to go there, little thinking what they will have to encounter. The picture looks bright at a distance but they have not seen it as I have — seen strong men break down under it and weep like children because of their inability to help themselves in the position in which they were placed. ... If they will not profit by the experience of others God help them I . . . I do not mind single men going, they can battle for themselves; but to send women and children is a crime. If I can persuade only one or two of the women not to go I shall feel that I have not striven in vain."

But all such warnings proved useless. William Lane's partisans had already explained away the secessions and such statements as those above were discounted in advance. On January 18th, 1895, thirty-one sailed . In all fifty or sixty more colonists were dispatched to New Australia and about; £300 in cash. As their passage money could not be raised, some two hundred destitute folk who had paid in their all to the Association, were left behind to accept charity from the much abused Capitalists and curse the day they had ever heard of Socialism. In the old days, when they so heartily endorsed the policy of confiscating the possessions of the well-to-do, they had never expected to be hoist with their own petard!

The Lane family house, New Australia Settlement

CHAPTER XIII.

THE ASSOCIATION TAKES TO BUSINESS.

While Casey was in Australia, hunting up fresh funds and re-establishing the recruiting base, the ever-changing officials in Paraguay were devising fresh schemes for frittering away each contribution as it came to hand. On all sides they were surrounded by magnificent forest, full of cedar, mahogany, teak, and other valuable woods, which only required to be chopped down, squared, and drawn by bullocks to Villa Rica or Caballero in order to produce an excellent revenue. Some idea of the possibilities of this trade may be gathered from the following notes of the use to which eleven of the sixty indigenous woods of Paraguay are put, together with the prices paid for them.

"(1) Curupai: A hard red wood, very durable and much used for sleepers, piles, etc. It commands a good market in the Argentine, the price in Asuncion being about 2S. the vara of 10 by 10 inches.
(2) Cedar: Though inferior in grain and scent to the Cuban variety, large quantities of this wood are exported to the Argentine Republic and to Germany, the trade with the latter country having sprung into existence at the time of the Spanish-American War. There is a considerable demand for Paraguayan cedar in Bremen, where it is used for the manufacture of cigar-boxes. It is, strictly speaking, more of a mahogany than of a cedar, but has the grain and scent of the latter. Price, 2S. per vara, 10 by 10 inches.
(3) Laurel negro (black laurel) is used for sleepers but not being

as durable as curupai and being inflammable the demand is not great. Price, is. 6d. per post.

(4) Palo de rosa (rosewood) is similar to the English rosewood but lighter in colour. Properly seasoned it takes a high polish and is suitable for light furniture. It also possesses medicinal qualities. Price uncertain.

(5) Ibirgno is a hard flexible wood for which there is a growing demand for carriage and ship-building as it does not warp or crack. Importers in the United Kingdom have expressed great satisfaction with samples received and state that it may replace teak to a great extent, the grain being very close and well adapted to resist the action of sun and water. Its one defect is its heaviness, but in spite of this there is reason to believe that it will soon command an increased sale in Europe. Price, about 2s. the vara of 10 by 10 inches.

(6) Lapacho (black and yellow): There is a great demand for this wood in Buenos Aires where it is used for making rough carts and spans for bridges. Though sometimes used also for sleepers it is not well adapted for this purpose, as, unless covered over with soil, it is apt to take fire from the sparks from the engine.

(7) Peteriby negro is used locally for furniture making, and being easily worked and capable of taking a high polish should, when better known, command a sale in Europe. Price, about 3s. the vara.

(8) Quebracho colorada, is the most important of Paraguayan woods, considerable quantities being exported to Germany chiefly to Hamburg, where a large amount is always kept in stock. Its principal use is for tanning, and the demand is increasing every year. German capital finds a remunerative investment in this wood, and a line of steamers is employed solely for this trade. There is one extract factory in this country, but probably several more will be established before long. The price of Quebracho Colorado delivered in Hamburg is about 66s. per ton. According to an analysis recently made Quebracho logs

produce an average of 25 per cent, of tanning substance and a maximum of 29 per cent. Paraguayan quebracho contains more tanning extract and is of a finer colour than that found in Argentine.

(9) Urundimi is one of the best hard woods of the country and possesses many of the qualities of the Curupai , being even more durable.. Price, about 2S. the vara of 10 by 10 inches.

(10) Tatana is a beautiful golden-coloured wood resembling satin-wood and taking a very high polish. Boxes made of it secure the contents from insects of all kinds. This wood is of a hard close grain and will last for years in the earth or under water. Locally it is used for making stems and sterns of ships. Price, about 2s. 4d. per vara of 10 by 10 inches.

(11) Palo Santo, Lignum-vitcei A heavy dark wood of which there is but a limited supply. It is used in place of bronzes for bearings in engines and screw shafts. Pulley and block wheels are also made of it. Palo Santo has the medicinal qualities of the Lignum-vita. Price, about £6 per ton in Asuncion. Hitherto it has been chiefly exported to France where it has been known to fetch £10 per ton."

In the vast forests on the 600 square miles which comprised the New Australia concession most, if not all, of the above were to be found in plenty, as well as dozens of other varieties of wood which enjoyed a local market. Indeed lumbering was the industry on which the prospectors had relied, in their report, for revenue, and it required no capital outlay to pursue it; nothing but hard work in fact — but this was a fatal qualification in the colonists eyes. For their own benefit any of them would cheerfully have undertaken the work (at present, under individualism, it is a staple industry), but none could see why they should sweat in the forest while others followed less arduous occupations. So the timber took care of itself for awhile and the Board of Management found pleasing amusement in experimenting with the planting of ramie, and bought a costly but inefficient machine to prepare the produce for the market. Ten acres were planted with the fiber (used in the production of imitation silk) and immense care lavished upon it in the hope of realising enormous profits. Needless to say this expectation was not realised and the whole thing proved a ghastly failure.

It might be argued that this result had nothing to do with the nature of Socialism, but was due to the stupidity of the Board of Management. Experience elsewhere justifies the conclusion, however, that such mad schemes have a fatal fascination for all 'reformers.' To quote the frank words of General Rossel, who commanded the French Socialist Army during the Communist rising of 1871:
"They study with good faith the works of those philosophical day-dreamers who promise them a Paradise on earth; they are desirous of suddenly transforming the organisation of labour... and three-fourths of their time they are the mere dupes of their infuriating merriments. Incapable of managing their own affairs, they are still more incapable of managing public affairs."

Besides the timber industry, there were many other avocations in which the colonists might have engaged with profit. They possessed 2500 head of cattle, in addition to 70 milk cows and 100 horses. Dairy-farming might have provided a useful income, while the fattening up of cattle for market would have yielded a splendid revenue. At the present time a dozen or more of the colonists, working for themselves make an excellent living at the trade, the Colony grazing land being unrivalled for this purpose. By extraordinary perversity, however, energy was concentrated upon market gardening, though there was no possible market for the produce.

The question whether proper care would be taken of common

property, under a Socialist regime, is one that Socialist writers answer confidently. "Only a lunatic would wantonly destroy a harvest," says the author of Merrie England, "unless he might thereby reap some personal advantage". That was not the experience of New Australia, for wanton destruction of harvests and reckless misuse of implements were common.

"There is absolutely no regard for common property," wrote 'Colonist' in the Pall Mall Gazette:
"Tools and implements are lost, mislaid or destroyed in the most disgraceful manner. At the Las Ovejas settlements last year the melon beds were trampled on by adults and children . Thousands were broken open and not one was allowed to come to maturity."

The wholesale loss or appropriation of tools was carried to such an extreme that when harvest time came there was nothing to reap with.
"In the farming department, the sight of a number of men and boys working overtime, snipping off the ears of wheat into a bag with table knives, in a field which averaged one bushel to the acre, was no less admirable as indicating heroic pluck than the picture of a gang of men raking rows of cornstalks with their hoe handles."
 The wheat of course was a failure, but the maize harvest was gloriously abundant, so much so in fact that the agricultural workers were unable to garner it without help. Naturally enough, they applied to the Board of Management for temporary assistance from other departments, but the strict Trade Unionists of the community were up in arms.
"What?" they cried. "Permit cattle drovers, or bottle washers, to lend a hand in the harvest field? Heaven forbid!"
"Well, if you take up that attitude, the farming section will insist on their eight-hour day and refuse to work a minute overtime.

Then the rain will come and the harvest will be ruined. The welfare of the community is at stake!"
Naturally enough this appeal conveyed nothing to them. Had it been their own corn they would have worked all night to bring it in, but as for the community — that was another story. As de Tocqueville remarks, "Individual interest is the indispensable incentive to labour and economy."
Having no incentive but the good of all, not a soul would life a finger to help, so the agriculturalists shrugged their shoulders and worked only their bare eight hours, with the result that much of Nature's bounty was smashed down by rain and abandoned to the pigs.

"For a long time sentiment was the ruling factor in New Australia, business being left in the back-ground; now both sentiment and business are in the background. For the moment there seems to be nothing but mutual distrust, greed, jealousy and unkindness," wrote Rogers in his Report. Then with truly Socialistic optimism, he adds, "But I do not think it is more than a passing distemper. Necessity will force attention to business and sentiment may then take its right place."

It was not long indeed before the Board of Management took to business — with disastrous results. For some time the colonists had been living on short commons, but nevertheless there was a heavy debt and the supplies of clothing, stores, etc., were well-nigh exhausted. There was no remunerative occupation in progress, and the stream of subscriptions from England and Australia, had dried up. The leaders were faced with two alternatives, (1) either they must absolutely set their people to some productive labour, such as lumbering, or (2) they must raise money from outside.

With tender regard for the weary muscles of Labour they chose the latter alternative, and actually gave away for a song their own people's chief means of livelihood. Characteristically, the contracts were rushed through by the business agent without the consent of the bulk of the colonists. A howl of dismay arose when the latter learned to what their trusted leaders had committed them.

As has been noted already, the colonists owned at one time 2500 head of cattle. These were distributed on different grazing grounds, and the heads of the farming department had the haziest idea how many remained. There was an impression that there should still be about 2000 without reckoning natural increase, and it was decided to dispose of half that number. "The contract was rushed through before the people had time to consider it, and as hurriedly carried out. The men of Loma Rugua had at once petitioned against it, but it was too late. The contract was for 1000 head at 13s. 6d. per head, calves up to two years being thrown in," stated Rogers in his Report. "The cattle were mustered, when, to the surprise of everyone, not a thousand head could be found! There were 928 sold, and some 1500 calves thrown in for nothing."

Evidently there had been a huge blunder and yet, owing to the disgraceful want of system, no one was responsible. The price at which they were sold was, I am told, ridiculous, as shortly afterwards the hides alone fetched that figure. Had the cattle been sold in small lots, it is reckoned that one-half of the number sold would have realised more than the contract.

Still more remarkable was the timber contract, dated February 6th, 1895. It was hardly in accordance with the original spirit of their scheme for the Board of Management to enter into a 'capitalistic' contract, giving a certain outsider the exclusive right of cutting timber on their territory for a period of three years for a ludicrously small consideration. Not till the contract was signed did they realise that the colonists were no longer entitled to conduct lumbering operations themselves. It seemed as if the Board were suicidally determined to cut themselves off from all possible sources of revenue.

"After careful thought, in the light of previous contracts and schemes," says Rogers darkly, "I am of the opinion that interests, other than those of the colony, were involved in the matter." It might be replied that, at any rate the contractor was under no obligation to consider the interests of the Colony.

When the disastrous effect of these two contracts became known there were those who did not hesitate to declare that they had been betrayed by their officials, and some came forward with a proposition very much like this, "what's the good of pretending to be Socialists any longer ? It only gives the cunningest ones the chance to feather their nests. Let's divide everything up while there is anything left to divide and turn Individualists — 'each for himself and the devil take the hindmost!'"

As will appear in the next chapter, brotherly love was now a byword. Envy, hatred and malice had taken its place, and the noble resolve to bear one another's burdens had given place to a policy of grab.

Cosme Colony group photograph

CHAPTER XIV.

ALL FOR ONE AND ONE FOR ALL.

The injustice of equal sharing between industrious and idle, skilful and good-for-nothing, did not obtrude itself particularly in New Australia's prosperous days, when fourteen bullocks were slain every week and money was abundant, but when increasing poverty made it necessary to revise the scale of living, and the lordly credit allowance was reduced to a meagre pittance, the glaring folly of such a scheme made itself apparent. There was a lean wiry giant named M for instance to whom hard labour was the breath of life. Axe on shoulder he would take himself off to the forest and bring tree after tree, with fibre hard as iron, toppling to the ground. Single-handed he made a bigger clearing in six weeks than half a dozen of the 'born tired' variety could accomplish in six months. His earning capacity as a woodman, even in Paraguay, where wages are low, would be several pounds a week. On the other hand, take a lounging argumentative waster like X, who was never much better than a' sundowner' in Australia, and whose scamped labour would be dearly paid for by his bare keep. Would any sane man argue that both were equally useful to the community? At New Australia no account was taken of physical or mental capacity, and consequently both types were served alike. As a result there was no incentive to industry, and the profit earning power of the community was reduced accordingly.

It should be noted that members were at liberty to eat at the common table at a certain agreed mess-rate (paid for by deduction from the credit value of their labour checks) or to draw food from the stores at a price fixed by a committee, and make their own cooking arrangements. Theoretically, all articles grown on the establishment had to be sold through the store, so that if a gardener ate some of the produce over which he tended, or a child picked a banana from the thousands which grew wild, they were robbing the community. In practice, therefore, though everything belonged to all, it was illegal for an individual to eat so much as a berry without first calculating its value and having it debited against him on his labour check. As money did not circulate, the endless complications attending all negotiations can be better imagined than described.

In this connection it is interesting to recall one of those amusing conundrums which Mr. Blatchford sets himself in 'Merrie England'. "Under Socialism," he asks, "who would get the salmon and who would get the red-herring?"
"Perhaps under Socialism," he replies, "the salmon might be eaten by those who catch it. At present it is not."

Substitute chicken for salmon and the answer held good at New Australia. Although the chicken belonged to the community as a whole they were seldom seen in the common-cook-pots. The fleet of foot and the dexterous in concealment, had this advantage over their mates, that they could catch the chicken — and many illicit meals were enjoyed by certain of the colonists which were not debited against them in the books.

By a revised agreement, dated May 21st, 1895, it was decided that all adult members were entitled to a reduced credit of 2s. 10d. per week, to spend as they pleased, with a supplement of 1s. per week which must be spent solely on necessary clothing. Out of this allowance there was small margin available for any enthusiast to spend on the purchase of priceless art treasures, but then, as Gronlund says:
"But really we do not suppose there will be any citizen in the

Co-operative Commonwealth, when some time has elapsed, who has got £20000 to squander on a bit of canvas, and none should deplore it."

What the New Australian citizens were more inclined to deplore was the fact that none had twenty shillings to replace a worn and tattered suit. As children were the care of the community, they also received an allowance, adjusted, not according to size or appetite, but according to age. All alike under the age of fifteen were allowed 6d. weekly for clothing, and a graduated amount for food. As children were maintained under the guardianship of parents, it followed that those of the latter who were blessed with a 'quiver full' drew very heavily on the community's stores, although they performed no more labour than the others.   This fact naturally created many heart-burnings.

Consider two concrete instances:
A man and wife with three daughters, aged 18, 16, and 2 respectively, and two sons aged 12 and 6, would draw 17s. 4d. worth of articles weekly from the common stock, and live comparatively in clover, although only the man did any profit-making work. On the other hand, five bachelor adults of M 's type and a hard-working boy of fifteen, with tremendous waste of tissue to be renewed, and brawny frames to be covered with clothing, would get only 17s. 10d. between them for a full week's arduous work. The family would naturally mess together; they could live well, be well clothed, and have a comfortable unused credit on the community's books put by for a rainy day. The six hard-working bachelors, on the contrary, would be so perilously near to starvation that they might be in danger of eating one another. They would not have even the consolation of knowing that the well-fed man's wife and grown-up daughter were helping things along by doing their (the

bachelors') washing. Bearing in mind that "Unless woman repudiates her womanliness, her duty to her husband, to her children, to society, to the law, and to everyone but herself, she cannot emancipate herself. Therefore woman has to repudiate duty altogether," many ladies simply repudiated their obligations and refused to do any communal work, though the regulation was that all washing must be divided up amongst the women.

"There is not a person here who could honestly tell you that he has not degenerated under these conditions," wrote Mr. A. Macdonald, "Communism certainly renders people more selfish. At the general dining table each has his private bottle of treacle, which he stows away between meals under his pillows or elsewhere as best he can; while quite a number carry their utensils to and from the table with them. Knives, forks, etc., have an amazing faculty for disappearing in a communistic settlement."

Another colonist, in a letter to the Pall Mall Gazette, bore out this statement, and touched upon a still more serious matter. After describing the wholesale wastefulness already quoted (Chapter V) he adds:
"There is no probability of education for half the children, and they have been sadly neglected. Some of the little ones may be seen limping around with their feet in a terrible state from neglect. The atmosphere of gross materialism is most deplorable in its effects. There is no doubt that people professing some faith are the most pleasant to live among."

Dreadful as this picture of the Godless Eden is, the settlers had not yet plumbed the abysmal depths of misery which they were destined to experience. Although it was estimated that if every male adult could earn £1 a year the colony would thrive and pay its way, even this humble achievement was beyond their powers. The knowledge that even the laziest drones would share in the fruit of their industry paralysed the energies of the most industrious. Soon all money was exhausted, next the stores were entirely depleted of their stock, and the commonest necessities of life were unobtainable.

The most devout believers in the Marxian faith might well be puzzled to account for the difference between Socialist theory and Socialist practice as exemplified at New Australia. Every soul had started by believing, with Gronlund:
"To go a little into details; Suppose they go to work and establish first of all, a normal day, say of eight hours, and pay the workers twice the wages which each one has been receiving on an average for the ten years immediately preceding. We have no doubt that the wages can be raised and the working day shortened, that much with perfect safety, considering the enormous advantages of Co-operative Industry."

Since, in the bad old "Capitalistic lands the frugal workman only gets about one-third of his earnings," it seemed obvious that the workers should be three times as prosperous at New Australia as in the old days. The fact was, however, that they had never before felt the pinch of want so grievously. Even the most industrious lived in a state of beggary. What was the explanation? Capitalists being eliminated, who, now, was robbing them of the fruits of industry? Evidently 'Society.' Referring again to that most illuminating work, 'The Co-operative Commonwealth,' it appears that Mr. Blatchford is wrong in thinking that "under Socialism he (the worker) would get all his earnings."
"A man is entitled to the full proceeds of his labour — against any other individual, but not against Society," says Gronlund. "Society is not bound to reward a man either in proportion to

his services, nor yet to his wants, but according to expediency."

What becomes of the surplus which Society under Socalism deems it inexpedient to distribute, Gronlund does not explain. It would have puzzled Marx himself, at New Australia, to track down the cause which kept the coffers both of Society, and of the most industrious individuals, empty, when, theoretically, they should have been full. Being well primed with the belief that any individual's adversity necessarily implies unjust profits on the part of some other individual, some of the profounder philosophers at New Australia became well-nigh addled in the effort to discover what mysterious being was laying up a fat bank balance from the surplus-value of their labour. It took them a long time to discern that, under Socialism, the interests of Society and the individual are opposed, and they actually eat up one another's profits.

In this predicament what were the New Australians to do? Of course they lost no time in applying to the ever-patient Paraguayan Government, which granted them a monthly subsidy of $800 (about £2o) to keep them from starvation. For the rest, they determined to make a great effort to attract moneyed recruits from Great Britain, altering the Constitution so as to extract a minimum contribution of £30 per head only, members paying their own passage-money, and having three months' grace before they need throw all their possessions into the common fund. Furthermore, they departed so far from the original scheme as to "offer grants of lands to individuals, or groups of individuals, not members of the Association, on terms to be arranged between such individuals and the Board of Management or its duly authorised agents."

This offer induced a body of Englishmen, including Z , to arrive at New Australia with the intention of founding a species of colony within the colony, but on the strictest Communistic lines. Of course their attempt failed, as all such attempts must fail when those who participate spend more time in discussing their theories than in hard work. It was not long before they broke up and most of them left the country. Being better educated than most of the original colonists and persuasive-tongued withal, Z, who remained, speedily became a dominating influence upon the settlement.

Until this time the principle of excluding coloured persons from New Australia had been strictly adhered to, but now Z began to urge his fellow citizens to vote for the inclusion of natives in the benefits of the colony — a step which followed logically enough from the belief in liberty, equality, and fraternity which all professed. In spite of what they had already suffered through listening to the eloquence of silvery-tongued orators, the New Australians were persuaded to agree, and the fiat went forth that natives should be allowed to settle on the Colony land.

It is all very well for theorists to argue that there is no difference between the coloured and the white man, except for the hue of his skin but those who have lived among natives know well that this is not so. The Qarani Indian of Paraguay is an amiable, indolent person, who is contented to sleep and smoke under the shade of his galpone, while his women folk work for him. Of garments he requires few: so long as he possesses a spirited horse, a good set of saddlery, and a properly obedient woman, he asks no more of fate. Incidentally, as he is not fond of formalities or permanent ties, he does not usually trouble to go through any legal form of marriage. The importation of natives into the New Australia Colony was the most fatal possible mistake; for the British boys and girls quickly foregathered with the natives, learned to talk the Guarani language, and, in the absence of any moral teaching from their own folk, grew to accept native ideals as their own.

A speedy result of the bringing of this new element into colony life was the fear which men now entertained of leaving their houses unprotected. The theorists, convinced that never a black heart beat beneath a dusky skin, at first pooh-poohed the suggestion that there might be any danger of robbery or other acts of violence by the natives, but they were quickly undeceived. O'Donnell, a married man, in charge of the store at Los Amigos, woke up one morning to find that natives had cut through the thatched roof in the night, and had moved the more valuable portion of the stock. This was only the first of many such troubles, which might have been avoided but for a too optimistic view of dusky human nature.

It was not long before even the enthusiast admitted that a mistake had been committed for the effect — upon the young bachelors in particular — of the introduction of a large body of Guaranis into their midst could not fail to produce the most deplorable effect on morals. As Mrs Mary Jane Gilmore wrote in the Sydney Daily Telegraph:
"The Paraguayans and the New Australians live side by side, equal under the law, and equal socially. The Paraguayan gives a dance and the white man attends it. The white man gives one and the Paraguayan comes. A wedding is the signal for an all-round drunk, Paraguayan and Australian drinking out of the same bottle. Everyone grows his own sugar and makes his own rum. So far, though there are half-caste children, there have been no marriages* with the Paraguayans."

Things had indeed reached a grievous pass at New Australia, and to make things worse the citizens of that 'ideal' state had now lost faith in their quondam principles. Their illusions gone, they had nothing to do but to sit in their mud huts, and endure their manifold miseries, with a hopeless feeling that they would have to put up with the same manner of living to the end of their days.

The Store at Cosme Colony

CHAPTER XV.

THE FOUNDING OF COSME COLONY.

The reader will recollect that the original pilgrims from Australia soon split off into three groups.

(a) The eighty-five seceders, who left 'New Australia' for the Gonzalez Colony in December, 1893, and were eventually repatriated, as related in Chapter X.

(b) The fifty-seven seceders who departed from 'New Australia with William Lane in the spring of 1894, as stated in Chapter XL.

(c) Those who remained at New Australia whose lamentable condition has just been dealt with.

The unhappy story of group A has already been concluded. The members of group B were left encamped beside a stream just clear of the New Australia territory. Abandoning group C to their miseries for the time being, the narrative will now return to the personal adventures of William Lane and those who seceded with him.

To the amazement of those who remained, William Lane's party marched out behind their leader, with superb confidence in him and in the future, although the funds they had in hand amounted to less than fifteen shillings per head. Their high spirits and lofty hopes are clearly shown in the following letter which one of the party sent to a friend in Adelaide.

"As to us poor exiles who are going," wrote Mr. H. S. Taylor, "you would never think us deserving of pity could you see us. We are the only happy people in the settlement; and we are happy (for we trust one another, and feel this time that we have reason for our trust), and we love and trust our leader; and together and with him we know we shall be happy anywhere. Fifty resolute men and untold wealth of experience; what shall we not accomplish therewith? For a short time we shall have rough living, of course, but what of that? In a few months we shall be ready to welcome the weakest and the feeblest... We are all in such excellent spirits at the prospect before us that many of the other party thoroughly believe that Lane has managed to steal a few thousand pounds somewhere; for to them, poor souls, it is absolutely inconceivable that men who are penniless should be happy."

During the ensuing two months the party had need of all their faith, for Lane's application for a further grant was not well received in Asuncion, where the authorities began to grow a little weary of the Australian immigrants' dissensions. Finally a grant was offered in the wild yerbales, where the matt, or Paraguayan tea, grows. Hearing that the site was only eighteen miles away the party set off at once to inspect it, but the intervening country was of such a description that the hardiest pioneer took ten days to traverse that short distance.
"The inspection showed that the grant was utterly unsuitable, being in wild, rugged country, with a sandy soil, and practically no communication with the markets. Another disadvantage was that it was Indian country. In the nearer distance lay part of the mountains of Central Paraguay, seamed, scarred and riven by great gorges, and inhabited only by wild animals — the jaguar, the puma, and the carpincho — to say nothing of the smaller fry — ocelots, tiger-cats, and others."

Desperately disappointed, William Lane hastened back to the

capital to beg the minister to grant more suitable land, but by this time the official's patience was quite worn out, and he intimated clearly that the party must take or leave what he had already offered. Almost in despair, Lane began to think of migrating to the Argentine, but a lucky circumstance provided an alternative. One of his followers, a man named Stevenson, received from Scotland a legacy of £150 which he at once placed at Lane's disposal. In addition it appears that a considerable sum of money was forwarded from New South Wales by Australian sympathisers. With his resources thus reinforced, William Lane approached a private land owner and negotiated the purchase of five and a half leagues of good land, only thirteen miles from a railway station, in the fork of two rivers — the Pirapo and the Tebicuari. Having received a deposit of £100 the owner agreed to accept the balance of £300 by instalments of £100 per annum. Feeling assured of his ability to attract to his new settlement most of those who had contemplated going to New Australia, Lane had no doubt he would be able to raise the necessary funds to complete the purchase, and his companions shared his optimism.

It would be difficult to exaggerate the sufferings of the little band, encamped beside a swollen river, without a roof to their heads, in the middle of the Paraguayan rainy season. It was the month of July, 1894, before negotiations were concluded. Rain fell in torrents as they entered into possession of their new land, which was christened Cosme Colony, and tramped through the waist-high grass in search of a suitable site to pitch two tents to give the women shelter. Yet the women patiently endured without a murmur, and the two little babes that were born in tents, in the middle of the wilderness, were hailed with rapture as the forerunners of the new and better generation. The first child born on Cosme territory was Cosma Lane, daughter of William Lane's brother, John. Though the outlook was not very bright, as yet, the fond parents believed that Cosme would have made its mark in the great world long before Cosma grew up.

Yet Cosme's heritage is free, each child is born
its heir,
And Labour lends its magic power that dowry
to adorn.
What though 'tis the wilderness I Loves knows
it fresh and fair.
We'll make it matchless heritage for babies yet
unborn.
For them the clearing-fires shall wave black
banners to the skies,
Bearing the struggling forest back to where the
rivers flow.
For them shall wind and water toil; for them
embankments rise,
For them shall English grasses spring where
Cosme's cattle go.

Thus one of them wrote. In all that they said and did the Cosme pioneers were acutely anxious to deserve the good opinion of futurity. The impatient word, the weary complaint, were hushed, so that future Cosmans might say with truth that the hard-ships which their forbears endured were nobly borne. While this spirit reigned, mere physical sufferings seemed of less than no account. 'It seemed like Heaven' after the mutual distrust and suspicion of New Australia.

It must have been a source of satisfaction to William Lane to know that his own wife and children had no such hardships to endure. After the first secession he had sent them back to Australia by the Royal Tar, giving Mrs. Lane instructions to proceed with the organisation of a party of single women. Thus she escaped the miseries which fell to John Lane's wife and family. Furthermore, her revelations concerning the state of affairs at New Australia hindered many from going there, although they were hardly calculated to assist in recruiting for Cosme.

Avoiding the errors of New Australia, the Cosmans set to work at once upon the essential task of ensuring next season's food supply. Even the women armed themselves with machetes, and accompanied the men into the forest, to aid in the strenuous work of clearing. It is a peculiar characteristic of Paraguay that crops cannot be induced to grow upon the clear grass land; the earth will only show itself bountiful towards those who clear away tall trees and matted jungle from its bosom. Once some rough shelter had been provided, no more time was wasted in building operations; from sunrise until they flung themselves down, dead-beat, at nightfall, the Cosmans fought the forest with axe, and machete. So soon as any patch was cleared of the denser growth, the soil was hoed over and sowed, for it was already late in the planting season, and ploughing must be postponed till the stumps and roots were got out, next year.

During the first six months the Cosmans allowed themselves only one relaxation — the compiling of a written witness of their unfailing cheerfulness for the edification of future Cosmans. This manuscript paper, magnificently titled Cosme Evening Notes, began to be published at once, and faithfully reflects the joys and sorrows of the settlers. After a day's severe toil in the monte, or the long pursuit of errant cattle which had strayed into the bigestero (swamp), the weary worker with a gift for rhyme would console himself and his comrades by a cheerful forecast of the days when Cosme would know such trials no more. The following doggerel 'Reflections,' scrawled by the blistered hands of one of the pioneers, on August 31st, 1894, indicate some of their trials and the hopes that spurred them on:

The big estero then we'll drain and bid farewell
to bogs,
Our houses we will build of stone instead of grass
and logs,
Mosquitoes then will disappear, the hornets too
will fly,
But the bees will bring us honey in the future by
and bye.
Our horses, sheep and cattle too will then the
world surprise,
And all our wants will be supplied just as those
wants arise,
So let us stick together boys; though now we're
but three score,
The future soon will see us grow to many
thousands more.

But for the great hopes which buoyed them up, it is probable that many of the Cosmans would not have survived the starvation and general miseries of that first six months. Every week, Lane's followers grew gaunter-faced and more hollow-eyed.

"In the store supplies ran down day by day till women washed without soap, cooked without fat, and patched the outer garments with the inner. Flour was almost non-existent. Every article of value that anyone possessed sooner or later found its way to Asuncion to be sold and the proceeds spent in buying kerosene, beans, salt, or maize. When things got very bad a tarpaulin muster brought in even wedding rings. Maize at last practically gave out. Light was available only in case of night nursings and in a day or two there was no salt," wrote Mrs. Gilmore in the Sydney Daily Telegraph.

"Meantime the long hours of labour went on. Spring passed and summer came. For two weeks the colony fed wholly on unsalted beans. Then the maize came in... immediately after mandioca followed then sweet potatoes and beans."

Never was a harvest more eagerly awaited. Even when it came, however, the diet was almost entirely vegetarian, and such things as flour, tea, butter, etc., were, of course, unobtainable. All the food was of the same 'starchy' variety.

"Being so starchy the amount of actual nourishment is small, while the varieties of indigestion they produce are severe and many. There is practically no fat. A housewife in my time thought herself lucky if she had a teaspoonful of fat in a month with which merely to grease the pan. And any man who got his food cooked with a taste of fat declared he felt stronger all day for it."

In spite of all such hardships, New Year's Day, 1895, found the Cosmans still a united family, principally perhaps, because all were so busy in warding off starvation that they had little appetite for meddling in politics. Meanwhile William Lane profited by his experience at New Australia to draw up a different constitution for Cosme Colony. And the first thing he decided to rule out was the suffrage of married women:

"We are often asked by outsiders why women in Cosme have no vote," wrote an educated Cosme woman to an Australian sister who possessed the vote. "Perhaps they think that we should have brought all the political and social evils of the time with us. They seem to forget that the 'voting woman' is only another form of the highly diseased state of city life. The Cosme woman knows that her position and welfare are too well assured to trouble her head about voting. Her governing powers are more in requisition in her immediate surroundings — her home. . . . May the question of women voters never arise in our colony, nor the need for the women to cope with the grasping sordid conditions of the competitive system of the outsider."

Another important difference between the constitution of Cosme and the original New Australian agreement referred to the arrangements for withdrawal. Anticipating that any hardships suffered by expelled and seceding members would form an effective deterrent to future recruiting, William Lane provided that a definite share of the common property could be claimed by any withdrawing members. The following is the text of The Cosme Agreement, as it stood in April, 1897.

The Cosme Agreement.
Villages: Cosme shall be divided into villages; each village having its own local authority, all villages being united under a central authority.

Each village shall elect three (3) committeemen yearly for a term of three (3) years; each village committee elect one (1) village executive officer yearly for a term of three (3) years; village executive to retire if they lose seat on committee; each village elect a village chairman for a term of three (3) years, village chairman to have previously served as executive officer; village chairman to be subject to suspension by a two-thirds majority of village committee.

Central Authority: The central authority shall be composed of a general chairman elected by general vote for a term of five (5) years, and a board consisting of all village chairmen and of one (1) delegate-committeeman from each village committee. The central authority shall appoint one (1) general executive officer yearly for a term of three (3) years, general executive officers to retire if they lose seat on board. The general chairman to have previously served on general executive, and to be subject to suspension by a two-thirds majority of the board.

Voter: The householder in good standing to be the voter in all village and general elections. Householders to be over twenty-one (21) years of age, and one (1) year's membership.

Functions: The functions of the central authority shall be the maintaining of Cosme principles, the holding of Cosme land, the holding and handling of the general funds, the establishing of new villages, the organising of co-operative action, and any other general functions which may by expressed consent or custom be assigned to it by the community at large.

The functions of the village authority shall be the maintaining of Cosme principles, the organising and directing of all village industry, the holding of all village property, the regulating of all village matters, the assisting of the central authority, and any other functions which may by expressed consent or custom be assigned to it by the householders of its village ; provided always that no function of the central authority, expressly or customarily approved by the community at large, shall be interfered with by any village authority.

All land shall be held by the central authority for occupation by Cosme villages. Improvements inseparable from the land shall not be evaluated for sharing purposes by any village, but in place thereof each village shall set from time to time, with the consent of the central authority, compensation to withdrawers based upon the working value of improvements. The control of natural grass, natural timber, natural water, and mines of every kind, shall always remain with the central authority.

General Funds: The general fund shall consist of a loan fund, an emergency fund, and an enlargement fund.

Each village authority shall pay into the general funds the value of one (1) day's work per week of the full working strength of the village. The central authority shall place this payment as follows : three fifths to the loan fund, one-fifth to the emergency fund, one-fifth to the enlargement fund. All other contributions, payments and donations, not otherwise specified shall be similarly placed. Contributions by members new or old, shall be returnable upon their withdrawing from membership less a yearly deduction of one-tenth of the original amount, such refund to be a first charge upon the general funds. The general funds shall not be otherwise liable to any claims by any withdrawing member.

Membership : Membership must be either by birthright or by admittance. No charge shall be made for membership, but no member shall have any interests outside of Cosme. All contributions to capital by incoming or other members to be placed in the general funds.

The children of members shall be registered as inborn members and shall be entitled to maintenance and education while minors, and to all membership rights when of due age, provided their parents continue in membership. The Cosme marriage age shall be after twenty-one for men and after eighteen for women. First cousins shall be regarded as within the forbidden degrees.

All admittance shall be through the central authority but any village authority may refuse entry to its village. There can be no Cosme membership without village membership, and no residence without membership.

Dividend: No dividend shall be made by any village until maintenance, education, sanitation, general fund payments, and other necessary expenses have been provided for. Any dividend made shall be allotted to all adults equally, by crediting each householder with an amount proportionate to the number of adults in his family. For the equalisation of the sexes in the village a levy of one-third shall be struck upon all dividends, which levy shall be suspended whenever the necessity ceases ; this levy shall be paid into the enlargement fund.

Withdrawing: Any householder withdrawing from Cosme shall be entitled to claim from his village a one-tenth withdrawal share for every year he has been a householder, up to ten (10) years; or, if inborn, shall be entitled to claim a one-fifth withdrawal share for every year over the age of twenty (20) up to five (5) years, provided that no inborn member withdrawing shall take more than a one-tenth share for each year he has been in Cosme. No withdrawing householder to claim more than a full share. The withdrawal share to be as arranged from time to time, at general village meeting with the consent of the central authority.

Children at Cosme Settlement, 1898

t

he reading of the 'Cosme Evening Notes'

CHAPTER XVI.

COSME RITES AND CEREMONIES.

When the first arduous rush of settlement work was over there followed a reaction at Cosme. It would be a very bad advertisement of the place, among outsiders, as the rest of the world was designated, if the Cosme community required sixteen hours toil daily of its members. At the earliest possible moment, therefore, the eight hour day was instituted, for men and single women, with the additional proviso that nobody should be required to work for the community more than four and a half days per week. There was nothing to prevent any citizen from doing additional work in private time, but it was expressly laid down that none should be done for profit except by order of, and for the benefit of, the community.

It might be supposed that the citizens would make use of their ample leisure to exchange useful work between themselves; those, for instance, who were carpenters by trade could make the homes of their neighbours more comfortable, in return for some equal benefit. There was very little voluntary interchange of service, however. Strange to say, many citizens were so jealous of doing more work for the community than their neighbours, that they forbore to improve their own residences unless told off for that purpose, as part of the building squad, during the ordinary working hours. As the community required to devote the whole of the working day to more productive labour, the rude and squalid mud huts, originally put up, long continued to serve as homes for all save a favoured few. In fact it was six and a half years after the first settlement at Cosme before the community so much as considered the question of providing each family with a tolerably comfortable home. (See Appendix E.)

No pen picture of Cosme could give a clearer idea of its life than the following extract from a letter, written home to his friends by an enthusiastic Scots recruit, when the settlement had been just over three years in existence :

"You can imagine a little village with rude huts for houses scattered here and there with no pretence to streets, the huts thatched with grass, with mud floors, and shutters for windows, with no showy furniture nor modern household conveniences. You can imagine a long building somewhat like a hay shed in the old country, with slab sides and boasting a wooden floor — this is the single men's dining room, and where all our meetings and socials are held. You can imagine at dusk a gruff voice roaring out Evening Notes and you can see men, women, and children strolling from their huts to hear Notes read at the dining room. Notes contains the news of the day, the work going on, interesting letters from friends and well-wishers, clippings from the latest papers, etc., etc. Then after Notes, you can imagine little groups of men discussing the news, or the work doing or to be done; and others playing chess or draughts or cards, until it is time to stroll home again to our own firesides. At half-past five in the morning we are disturbed from a peaceful slumber by the deep sound of a horn, this reminds us that we might as well be getting up, at six o'clock another horn tells us our breakfast is ready, and at half-past six another horn reminds us that there is some work to do, and each one then goes to his day's toil. At half-past eleven the dinner horn goes, and the work horn again at half-past twelve, whence we work on till four o'clock, when we finish for the day."

It will be observed that the same people who argued that it was slavery under Capitalism for the factory hand to commence and finish work to the sound of a hooter, submitted tamely enough under Socialism to rising, breakfasting, working and even pleasure-making to the sound of a horn. But then, as the writer of the above letter remarked, "the theoretical Socialist has very little idea what it means to go out into the wilderness to put his pet theories into practice. There are a thousand little details he has never thought of. He finds that human nature doesn't change with new conditions."

William Lane had made that discovery too. Whether consciously or not, and in spite of constitutional safeguards, he managed his docile flock in almost precisely the same fashion as the Jesuits controlled their Indian communities in Paraguay.

Although the Deity, as Christians know Him, had no place in the Cosme scheme, Lane realised the necessity of a theocratic domination if he would carry his scheme through. But what god should he set up; having dethroned Christ from His place?

"No fault of his is it if, of this strange and tearful teacher, heathens have contrived a strange and tearful god," William Lane preached to his flock at Christmas, 1898,"nor if his simple story has been overlaid by juggled legends, and twisted into pretentious framework for blasphemous oratory It is clear that Jesus, like Tolstoi today, never understood the healthy physical life, and so expounded an unbalanced philosophy."

Lane of course did understand the healthy physical life and was therefore qualified to expound a properly balanced creed. From his brief experience at New Australia Lane discovered that under pure materialism, with no lofty ideal for a guiding motive, his people could not fail to degenerate. Furthermore, he discerned the immense assistance which statecraft derives from religion, since the latter encourages to good conduct from other motives than mere fear of the policeman. He therefore decided that Cosme must have a religion after all.

Just as he had emulated the majestic figure of Moses in leading the New Australians forth from Australia, so Lane copied him again in producing (though with no better inspiration than his own ingenious brain) a complete system of religion for his flock to follow. From the time he took that resolution the Cosmans could not boast that they escaped the preacher in their ideal community. Lane was continuously 'at it,' preaching the Law of Communism under which, like the Israelites under the Mosaic Law, Cosmans got short shrift for heresy.

"I will state to-night, as clearly and as shortly as I can, the way of thinking which makes me a Communist," said Lane in one of his Sunday evening sermons, "When I say Communist, I do not mean merely one who accepts theoretically certain theoretical or even ethical conceptions of Society, but one who holds that the practice of Communism is absolutely necessary to make life natural, wholesome and happy, and that it is the bounden duty of man, even by himself, to try ceaselessly and in spite of his own shortcomings to put Communism into loving practice in his life. With me that belief springs from an absolute and unshakeable faith in what we commonly call 'God.' And when I say God I mean neither the idol built of wood or stone by the crude hands of savages, nor the idol built of words and phrases by the equal heathenism of higher races. I mean by God the sense of the oneness, the lovingness, the completeness of that inconceivable power which, working through matter called us, and all the wondrous universe we see, into being. That power I know and feel is supreme beyond all conceiving. Nothing is beyond its control. ... In all the universe, in the whole earth, there is none but God who rules — One God and no other. . . .

"But one may ask, what has Communism to do with belief in God. This: that to me Communism is part of God's law. ... He who with all his heart and soul endeavours to be Communist of himself, freely, and to mould upon Communistic lines the social organisation without which man cannot live on earth, he is, in so far serving God and obeying God's law. And he who does other is sinning, is wilfully and deliberately setting his own petty desires against God. . . . Communism, the brotherliness in society of man, is to me a part of God's law. Death comes to those who deny it. Misery and sorrow fill the world because we will not obey...

"All this Law we do not know as yet, and much must Man suffer ere he learns it all and understands what indeed he is. But parts of this Law we know and know clearly... And Communism is a part of the known and certain Law of things. Never great teacher taught these ages back who did not teach so. As I hold and believe; God laws it."

The obvious advantage of such a system of theology in a Communistic State is, that any citizen who dares to criticise Communism brands himself at once as the enemy of 'God' and man, and it is nothing less than the bounden duty of the authorities to eject him. By elevating his pet theories from a mere political creed to a revealed religion, with himself as executive High Priest, to criticise whose decisions would be little less than blasphemy in the eyes of his most faithful adherents, William Lane set up a powerful barrier to the disruption of his new community by internal factions. In order to facilitate the ejection of intractable citizens from Cosme, Lane inaugurated a system of 'trial membership,' whereby no recruit had a vote until he had spent a year on the settlement and had proved his suitability. Any prospective citizens who wished or were ordered to withdraw before the expiration of the probationary period were allowed to leave with their possessions intact.

To impress upon newcomers the serious nature and aims of 'Cosmeism' a ceremony of initiation was also instituted. Prior to the public reading and signing of the membership certificate, and of the Mutual Agreement, by colony officials, new members and witnesses, the chairman read the following exhortation to the assembled citizens:

"For the well-being and healthy growth of Cosme it is needful that we be joined by people of our own race who are one with us in thought and purpose.

"Only by increase of membership can Cosme realise the object of its foundation, make complete and self-sustained its industrial development, make broad and deep its social life, and prove to the world that brotherly living is both possible and practicable to earnest people.

"The taking and giving of the pledge of fellowship is no light matter. The endeavour to live up to the spirit of that fellowship, demands from each one of us, deep resolve, constant thought, persistent effort and unfailing patience. The human failings and weaknesses inherent in all of us must ever hinder perfect living. But knowing these weaknesses, we can if we will, so guard against them that in spite of stumbling we may keep moving forward.

"Above all things it is needful that we cherish in our hearts the spirit of brotherhood which is the very soul of fellowship, that it may influence us in all our doings, keeping us from selfishness and strife, and leading us ever in the path of peace and goodwill towards that fellowship of heart and mind which passeth understanding"

The reference to social life serves as a reminder that this was the feature above all others on which William Lane most strongly insisted. Every evening at the sound of a horn, the people assembled to hear the reading of Cosme Evening Notes, each Saturday night the same folk met for a 'Social' and danced together under the benevolent eye of their master, with at least affected enjoyment, although they had worked side by side all the week and had danced the same dances together some scores of times before. On Sunday nights there was a further meeting in the 'Social Hall,' where an oration by William Lane, or reading from standard works on Socialism took the place of any orthodox form of religious service. The following extract from the Cosme Monthly, for June, 1897 (when the resident population was 57 men, 22 women, and 35 children), conveys a clear idea of the settlement's social life:

"May 1 2th, Cosme's 'Foundation Day, was a public holiday. There was a communal dinner at mid-day, very successful sports in the cricket oval in the afternoon, and theatricals and dancing at night. The piece staged was a farce entitled, 'Blarney.' On the 29th, was a special wedding social on the occasion of the second Cosme marriage. The ordinary Saturday socials were carried on as usual, as also were the Sunday night meetings. Among readings given at the latter were: Hall Caine's 'Christian' (three chapters), Nunquam's 'New Religion,' Clodd on 'Buddhism', two sketches by Price Warung, various short articles and some letters from absent members. Songs and glees were also sung. The Spanish and singing classes are going on steadily, many of the new members having joined, there now being 19 in the former, and 26 in the latter. The musical instruments have been increased by two violins, a banjo, and a harmonium. This last instrument was brought in by Arthur Lewis and is at the service of the social union. Sports: There has been a little fishing indulged in with moderate success. The hunters occasionally brought home small game. A little cricket was played."

The wedding referred to above was that of Mrs. Gilmore (whose accounts of life at Cosme have several times been quoted). As has been noted already, William Lane differed from many Socialists on the marriage question. At Cosme couples were not merely united by the civil contract; there was also a religious service. As was only to be expected the latter differed as much from any hitherto existing service as the Cosme religion differed from other creeds. It is probable that never before in history did so small a community (its adult population never totalled one hundred) trouble to provide itself with an original marriage ceremony. The following was the exact text of the:

Cosme Marriage Service.
The bride and bridegroom being present with their parents or other witnesses in open meeting, the official representative of Cosme says:

"For the lasting life of any people, it is needful above all things, that its men and women be honest. For although there may sometimes seem to be welfare without honest living, yet sooner or later, in one way or another, evil doing utterly destroys. Marriage therefore, is holy if we take it rightly, being the public declaration by man and woman of their going to live together as man and wife, in accordance with the laws of God; and of their acknowledgment on behalf of themselves and of the children who may be born to them, of the duties which they and theirs owe to the people.

"Wherefore, this man and this woman, members of Cosme, have come before us all to make that public declaration which is right and fitting, and to take again upon themselves those duties and obligations which give to them and to those who may be born to them, rightful claim to the standing Cosme pledges to all those who abide by its principles, and to enter into that civil contract of marriage, which, without taking from the holiness of the marriage state, makes their marriage according to the law of Paraguay.

"But first, as has been the custom with our people, if there are any here who know of good cause why the marriage should not take place, I call upon them to declare it now, or for ever after to hold their peace."

The bride and bridegroom then stand up in front of the meeting and the representative of Cosme then says to them:
"If any take upon themselves the duties and obligations of marriage, knowing that for any cause whatsoever they are unable to do so honestly and truly, their pledge is a mocking to all, a shamming of one who trusts them, and a breaking of the laws of God, Wherefore, so that you may shun in time the suffering that fails not to follow sin, I ask you each, severally, if you know of any cause why you should not marry?

"It is moreover a sinful thing for any man or woman to enter into marriage save for love only, since we are not as brute beasts, but are men and women with human feelings, which we must keep pure and undefiled, lest we debase and degrade ourselves. In Cosme there can be no fear of want, nor greed of gain, nor any unnatural pressure to excuse the weakest for so sinning. Wherefore, I ask you each, severally, if it is of your free will and choice that you come to pledge yourselves in marriage, knowing that the pledge is for life and that without true love, marriage is sinful, bringing a curse and not a blessing?

"In the outer world many dare not marry, because of the want and fear which have been born of men and women caring for themselves alone, and having no thought for others. Therefore because Cosme enables you to marry honestly, and without fear, I call upon you to pledge continued loyalty to Cosme, in prosperity or in adversity, and that you will teach its principles in your family and will always maintain them, and that you will work for and cherish your fellow-members and their families, as they work for and cherish you and yours."

The man and the woman repeat after the representative:
"We solemnly pledge ourselves to be loyal to Cosme in prosperity or in adversity, and that we will teach its principles in our family and will always maintain them, and will work for and cherish our fellow-members and their families, as they work for and cherish us and ours."

The representative then says to the meeting:
"You have witnessed the pledges given by and to Cosme, and to you as part of its people. I call upon you to join, by standing, in the pledge of Cosme, to be repeated to them in return. To you and at this your marriage, I repeat in the name of Cosme the pledge already given to you by your membership. To you for your life, in your sickness as in your health, in our prosperity as in our adversity, due place among our people, ever to try to do to you and yours as we would have you to do to us and ours. To your children all love and care and equal maintenance, during your life, or after your death; and upon their coming of age, full and free membership, provided only that you keep truly the pledge you have given, and that your children are likewise loyal."

The representative then asks of the bride and bridegroom respectively:

"Will you take this man (or woman) to be your husband (or wife) in all honesty and truth, pledging yourself before God, whom none can deceive, to be true wife (or husband) to him (or her) as long as you both live?"

The bridegroom then repeats after the representative:
"I take to be my wife and have my name, and do pledge myself before God, to be true husband to her as long as she lives, and I give her this ring as token of our pledge,"

The bride repeats:
"I take to be my husband and to have his name, and do pledge myself before God, to be true wife to him as long as he lives, and I take this ring as token of our pledge."

The representative then says:
"I declare this woman married to this man, and that she is his wife before all from this time forward."

The representative says to the meeting, in conclusion:
"In the name of Cosme I accept as married, and to be so entered in the books. I call upon every man here to show by rising, that he accepts this woman as a married sister, to be held as such at all times while her husband lives, and to be guarded as one of his own kin. And I call upon every woman to show, by rising, that she accepts this man as a married brother, to be held so at all times while his wife lives. And I call upon all, by raising our hands, to pledge ourselves not to wrong them, nor let wrong be done to them, and to join in casting out any evil-doer so that our marriages be kept unbroken, and so that our people may have God's blessing, and may live and not die."

Here immediately follows the Civil Contract of Marriage.

CHAPTER XVII.

RECRUITING FOR COSME.

In building the foundations of his ideal State William Lane was faced with a number of pressing problems, of which perhaps the chief was the need for securing against loss of the land on which it was established. During the first two years the necessity for scraping together the annual installments was a cruel anxiety, and cast a shadow over the lives of the responsible officials. But, after giving the Cosmans two years in which to prove their mettle, the authorities in Asuncion came to the rescue in their usual generous fashion. On June 25th, 1896, the Government paid the balance of the purchase money £200 still owing to the vendor, reimbursed to the Cosmans the money they had already paid £200, and made them a free gift of the territory and of another league besides. The only condition attached to the grant was that seventy-two families must be settled upon the land within two years.

This repayment of a comparatively large sum of money was a welcome boon, at a time when the Cosmans were reduced to sore extremities for want of various articles they were themselves unable produce. It should be explained that stores of all kinds were distributed to the settlers through a system of credits. Each individual was furnished with a card, on one side of which (a) or ' inside' credits were recorded, and on the other side (b) or 'outside' credits. 'Inside' credits referred to food, and articles of all kinds produced upon the settlement, 'outside' to imported articles, such as clothing, soda, salt, soap, matt (Paraguayan tea), etc. Supplies of all kinds, equitably priced, were issued by the store, equal credits being allowed to all adults, while children enjoyed a quarter credit for each five years of age. According to the original scheme 'inside' credit balances were extinguished every month, while 'outside' were cumulative; but the consequence of the latter regulation was that, in course of time, some frugal members were owed considerably greater supplies of 'outside' stores than the community could pay them. In fact, had it not been for the voluntary cancellation of their credits by some members the store would have become bankrupt. The immediate result of the Government's generosity was to restore Cosme's purchasing power, so that the com- plicated (a) and (b) system was replaced by an amalgamated credit, which gave much greater satisfaction (until, two years later, want of funds compelled a return to the old 'inside' and 'outside' distinction.

Two other difficulties confronting William Lane proved less easy of solution; these were (1) the immediate necessity of introducing a great many more immigrants, in order to comply with the Government's condition that seventy-two families should be settled within two years, and (2) the fact that there was a serious disproportion between the number of adult men and women at Cosme. As the former outnumbered the latter by nearly three to one there was no immediate prospect of matrimony for two-thirds of the bachelors, and William Lane very much feared that the temptation to take wives from among the graceful, docile, and industrious native women would prove irresistible.

The obvious way to meet both difficulties was to start forthwith upon a vigorous campaign of recruiting, restricted, so far as possible, to families (a married couple form a family within the meaning of the Paraguayan law) and single women. Since there were already fifty men and twenty women at Cosme, it would only be necessary to recruit thirty single women and twenty-two married couples to redress the balance, hold the young men to the place by family ties, and comply with the Government conditions for the final, unconditional, surrender of the titles to Cosme land.

William Lane had not the slightest doubt that scores of recruits could be found in England, only too eager to shake off the shackles of Capitalism and bid for a share in Cosme bliss. He was anxious, however, that no new members should join who were not thoroughly imbued with the proper Cosme sentiment, and prepared to submit with docility to the existing regulations. He, therefore, determined to make a personal visit to the United Kingdom, accompanied by his lieutenant, Tozer, for the purpose of sifting the wheat from the chaff, and forwarding only such candidates for membership as satisfied his exacting requirements. The two organisers sailed in September, 1896, intending to enrol and dispatch some fifty members before March, 1897, when Lane would return, leaving Tozer to keep the propaganda going for a few months longer. In addition to making arrangements for assisted passages, the Paraguayan Government gave Lane the hospitality of their London Consulate, where a Cosme Colony Agency was established.

Immediately on his arrival in England, William Lane put himself in communication with the Labour and Socialist organisations of the United Kingdom, and arranged for a whirlwind campaign of meetings and lantern lectures in the chief industrial centres. The years which had elapsed since he first projected his 'ideal' Commonwealth had to some extent tempered his optimism, but by no means quashed his enthusiasm. The prophet of the new movement who addressed himself to British democrats was mellower and more restrained than the fiery young journalist who formerly swayed the Australian public, but his appeal was all the more likely to succeed on that account. Up and down the country he preached Cosmeism to sympathetic listeners, but took great care to emphasise the hardships inseparable from pioneering, in order that none might claim that he had lured them to Paraguay by false pretences.

It would serve no useful purpose to follow Lane's itinerary, or multiply examples of his burning oratory. Suffice it to say that he met everywhere with a cordial reception, but failed to enlist the practical support of any strong body of advanced Socialists for a very definite reason — his obstinate insistence on the old-fashioned sanctity of the marriage vow. Though only too logical in accepting all the other consequences of Socialism, his 'irrational' opposition to the communalism of wives kept a wide gulf fixed between him and many other extreme Socialists, who but for that reservation would cheerfully have followed him. On the other hand drawing-room Socialists, while applauding his retention of the institution of marriage, recoiled from his logical application of the extremer view in other directions.

His disillusionment found expression in the report he sent back to the Cosme Central Board:

"Little help is to be expected from any school of advanced thought. This, because those schools which agree theoretically with our industrial methods are more or less opposed to our other ethical principles, while the old-fashioned people, who agree generally with our other ethical principles do not endorse those principles which aim at fundamentally reforming industrialism. At the same time much sympathy and fellow-feeling for us exist among individuals attached to most of the recognised schools, and many others, while not going all the way with Cosme, recognise that it has a distinct value as an earnest effort to solve the great social problem. In addition to meeting with fellow-feeling from many who already profess radical thought, Cosme will find fellow-feeling among many who are in reality radical, but who have been excluded by their conservatism on some ethical principles, from allying themselves with advanced thought as generally presented."

This does not mean of course, that his recruiting effort met with no result. In spite of his careful weeding out of all unsuitable applications, he was able to dispatch a number of prospective settlers, who satisfied him that they would make good Cosmans, but as the tally was still incomplete he decided to remain another year in England, and dispatch additional small parties from time to time.

The most interesting feature of the English and Scottish organisation was the reception which Lane's own recruits received at the hands of those temporarily in charge at Cosme. If he supposed that, because he had selected them, the new arrivals would find favour in the eyes of his original flock, he was grievously mistaken.

In spite of the universal equality they professed, the pioneer 'foundation' members not unnaturally regarded themselves as a sort of professed order of Cosmeiasm, towards whom mere novices should show due humility. If there were any choice as regards the quality of housing accommodation the newcomers did not get the best, being told that, "if they did have to rough it a little they might well be thankful that others did the pioneering." Furthermore, since the pioneers had hitherto done
all the 'hard graft,' it was quite reasonable that the more unpleasant tasks should be tackled in future by the raw recruits; but, however just such arrangements might be, it was only natural that the new arrivals should feel dissatisfied. On the other hand, if the management committee displaced an old

member from some task he liked, in favour of a more skilful British recruit, it was the former's turn to feel aggrieved.

It was between the ladies, however, that the most serious friction arose. It was at least four years since most of the Cosme women had entered a shop. During that period they had battled nobly for the 'Cause,' many of them working daily in the forest, where thorns tore their clothes in shreds; and grinding poverty had made it impossible for their tattered rags to be replaced. Any decent garments which still remained were reserved for such special occasions as the Saturday evening socials; in the ordinary way, even such elementary necessities as stockings were not worn, and many elected to go barefoot in preference to wearing the boots of home tanned leather which the community supplied. At any time it required a considerable fund of philosophy to endure such deprivations with any show of cheerfulness, but when newcomers from England appeared upon the scene, fashionably attired from head to toe, and with enough good clothes in reserve to last a year or two, there came a crisis.

The love which the Cosme ladies had been prepared to extend to their newly arrived sisters turned to gall and wormwood, and bitter reproaches were heaped upon the latter's innocent heads.

It was stated in a later issue of the colony's monthly paper: "Nobody with any sense of justice, much less of Communism, would dream of outfitting to any extent for such a place as Cosme. However little newcomers may have they are sure to have more clothing, bedding, and tableware than are left to the founders of Cosme after five years' pioneering. We have savings in the shape of improvements, machinery and cattle only because for years we have been pinching ourselves in food, clothing, and creature comforts. For people to expect to share our savings, after spending their own on special personal outfitting, is quite wrong. We do not wish for that class of people."

But the bitterness which found expression in cold print was as nothing to the acute division that showed itself between the sprucer and more tattered individuals. As was only natural the feeling found vent in a variety of ways, which could not fail to make the newcomers miserable, and some of them wished they had never left a country where to be well dressed is not accounted a crime. In this connection it is interesting to note the kind of tasks which were allotted to the newlv recruited Cosman ladies. Some light is thrown on the subject by the following official announcement:

"The single men's washing and mending, up till now done by the married women, has been mostly taken over by the new Laundry and Sewing Department organised early in October when the single women arrived. This department consists at present of two members."

It is possible that the ladies in question may have considered it a peculiar privilege to be told to undertake this work, but the reflection suggests itself that 8000 miles is a long journey to take in order to become unpaid slaves of the wash-tub.

Since so much unpleasantness existed, it was not surprising that secessions of men and women from Cosme commenced within a week of the first English recruit's arrival. The following record, condensed from 'Cosme' speaks for itself:

March, 1897. Arriva : Alf Bray, the first member from England, arrived on the 14th.

Departure : A. Mc.C, who was accepted as a member in January, resigned membership on March 18th, the reason assigned being that the climate of Paraguay did not agree with his health.

Present Population: Fifty-three men (including two absent on leave, and two in England on Cosme business), twenty women, thirty-one children. Total 104.

April, 1897. Arrivals: The first of the monthly parties from England arrived on the 16th. The party consisted of: Arthur Lewis, a mason from Stockport; Mrs. Lewis and one child; George Pridmore, a carpenter from Leicestershire; James Ricketts a carpenter from London.

Present Population: Total 109.

May, 1897. Arrivals: On the 25th, the second party from England arrived. They consisted of: Cyril Allen, gardener from Nottingham; Harry Buckley, ex-soldier from Macclesfield; Sidney Cash, deal-worker from Birmingham; John M. Parish, wood-carver from Bradford; Robert Rayner, warehouseman from Huddersfield; Nicholas Vallance, postman from York.

On the 22nd, Thomas and Mrs. Burgum, and three children arrived from Queensland.
Departures: On the 25th, G. W. P and J. R, both newly arrived from England, resigned membership.

Present Population: Total 118.

June, 1897. Withdrawal: On the 25th, R. W. R, a new English member, resigned.

July, 1897, Withdrawal: Writing from South Australia, H. S. T, a foundation member absent on leave, notifies that he will be unable to return to Cosme on account of domestic reasons.

Present Population : Total 118.

August, 1897. Withdrawals: On August 6th, J. A , W. M. and Mrs. M left Cosme. (All old members. Ill-health given as reason for leaving.) T. Burgum and Mrs. Burgum and family left the colony on August 9th.

September, 1897. Arrivals : On the 4th of September, from Edinburgh, William and Mrs. Titilah, and five children. W. Titilah is a bootmaker. Alice Clark (age 15) from London. Membership was refused to two arrivals from Scotland.

Present Population: Total 119.

October, 1897. Arrivals: On October 6th, the fourth British party arrived at Cosme. The new members are: George Gumm from Somerset, Georgina and Annie Noon from Hawick.

Present Population : Total 122.

December, 1897. Withdrawals: On December 21st, E. T and his nephew N. V left Cosme. (E. T was a pioneer member. He gave as his reason for going that he found that he was not a Communist. His nephew, who only arrived from England in May, left to keep him company.)

Present Population : Total 129.

January, 1898. Arrivals: On January 31st, William and Mrs. Bennett arrived from Australia.

Withdrawals : On January 8th, S.C and G.G, and on the 20th, A. W.L with wife and child, left Cosme. All were English recruits and found Cosme life unsuited to them.

Present Population: Total 127.

February, 1898. Withdrawals: On February 10th, A. B, a young English member, left on account of his unsuitableness for Cosme life. On the 12th, C. B , a junior, preparatory to his parents withdrawing. The Miss T 's, who arrived from England on February 5th, left for Buenos Aires on the 10th, they not being satisfied enough with the place to apply for membership.

Present Population : Total 125.

April, 1898. Arrivals: On April 8th, Robert Ogilvie, wife and two children; George Holland, Annie Ashton, from England.

Present Population: 53 men (including five absent on leave), 27 women, 46 children. Total 126.

*May, 1898. Departures: At beginning of month, J. B and wife, R.O, wife and two children, recently arrived from Scotland. Towards end of month, H. B, wife and one child; J. P, wife and three children ; J. A. S, wife and two children; *F. B, G. B, *C. B, G. C, G. H, L. P, *P. P, *H. S, *J. W. Those marked (*) were with the pioneers. Early in the month J. T. W left on leave of absence.*

Present Population: 39 men (including six absent on leave), 22 women, 38 children. Total 99.

A glance at the above statistics reveals that there were actually a dozen fewer adults at Cosme at the end of May, 1898, when the great recruiting campaign was over, than in March, 1897, when the first English member arrived. Moreover in June two absent members resigned, while, on July 1st, 1898, eight more left, including Lane's ever-faithful lieutenant, Arthur Tozer, with his wife. At the beginning of July, 1898, there were only 30 men, 20 women, and 36 children left at Cosme. It is true that six more men were 'absent on leave' but that usually proved a euphemism for withdrawal.

The cause of the earlier departures has been indicated already. The big secession in May, however, was directly due to the fact that William Lane had just returned from England and reassumed the reins of power. He was welcomed back by 121 persons, but within a few weeks there were only 50 adults and 36 children left upon the place. Yet this by no means caused the leader to be cast down, for, horror of horrors! he discovered that during his eighteen months absence the rank weed of heresy had grown up in the fair garden of Cosme. A considerable body of feeling had arisen in favour of altering some of his best loved regulations. It was the story of New Australia over again; and Lane no more hesitated now as his proper course of action than he had faltered then. Whatever the cost, any person who held less than the true milk of the Gospel of Cosmeism must be thrust out from among the congregation.

In anticipation, perhaps, of possible trouble with the newcomers, the last Cosme General Meeting (May, 1897) had been induced to grant exceptional powers to their elected committee of nine persons. It did not then occur to the voters that the innocent sounding resolution that a "two-thirds majority of the committee, with the consent of the village chairman, shall be necessary for the expulsion of a member" would, when that committee's mandate was within four days of exhaustion, be used against themselves.

The Annual Cosme meeting for the election of committeemen, etc., was due to be held on May 13th, 1898. On May 9th, William Lane and his nine existing committeemen met "to take action for the maintenance of Cosme principles." By their unanimous decision two members were expelled from membership for "antagonism to, and violation of, the Communist principles of Cosme." This action was promptly challenged by a considerable proportion of the eighty adults on the settlement, but alas from one disability and another, there were only twenty-seven full-fledged voting members on the place (including Lane and committee), and those upheld the expulsion by 19 votes to 6. As an immediate consequence those voting against the motion resigned and, with many of their voteless sympathisers decided to withdraw. By a curious coincidence this decision was taken upon Foundation Day — the fourth anniversary of Lane's own secession from New Australia.

Thus the expensive organisation campaign in England proved more than a failure. It was a catastrophe. After its conclusion Cosme was left numerically weaker than before; of the 15 men Lane had personally recruited in Britain 11 had already left, and of the 10 single girls only five remained. In addition, he had lost the adherence of some of the best of his original stalwarts. His must have been an iron resolution indeed, if the wreckage of so many lives by Cosmeism occasioned no wavering of his personal faith in it.

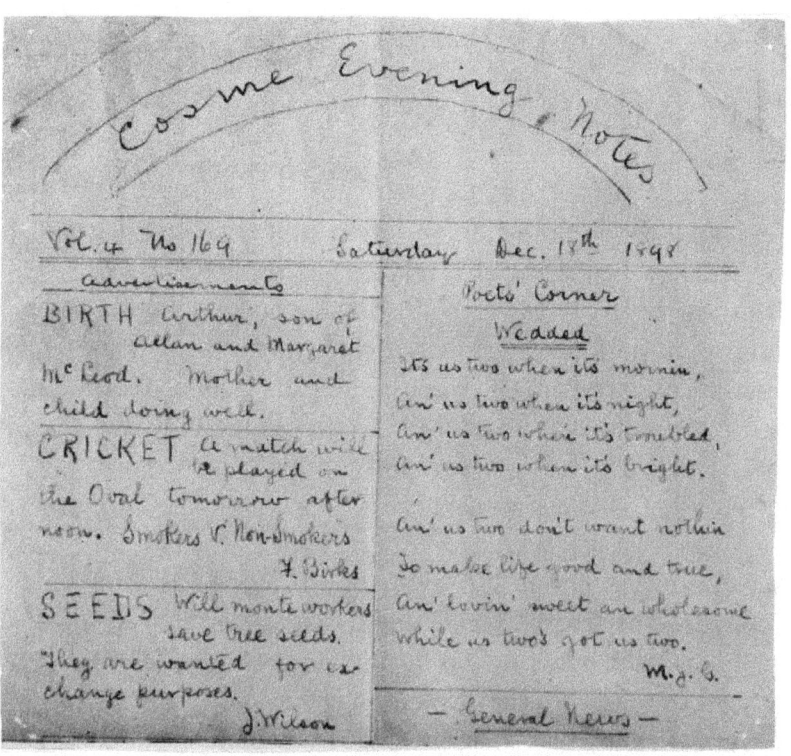

The Cosme Evening Notes

CHAPTER XVIII.

EXIT WILLIAM LANE.

The failure of the British organisation, and the dismissals and secessions which followed it were responsible for much bitterness of spirit at Cosme. Moreover the Paraguayan authorities' patience was stretched to the breaking point, when they saw depart from the colony a considerable proportion of the people whose passages from Monte Video they had paid only a few weeks before. Yet Lane continued to profess absolute faith in his own scheme:

"We dream our dream still, even though among us some have grown tired of dreaming and would wake again to that so-called reality in which every man is against his brother and nothing is thought of much worth, saving things material. Yet we have chosen not to be wakened but to go on dreaming still that Communism is a possible thing to try after, though doubtless a very impossible thing to fully attain to at once."

As time went on Communism was found increasingly difficult 'to fully attain to.' The resentment aroused in the breasts of some of the old-timers by the arrival of newcomers, with ampler supplies of good clothing, has been recorded. Such feeling was to some extent appeased by the voluntary sharing out of feminine fripperies, but the question of the clothing allowance was bound to recur from time to time and cause heart-burnings. At last disputes became so frequent that the regular clothing credit was abolished, and the principle "to each according to his need," established in its stead. It was arranged that any woman who required additional garments made formal application at the store, but soon the demand became so excessive that it was evident some sort of censorship would have to be exercised. The unhappy storekeeper found himself compelled to solve at short notice such problems as "Does Mrs. really need a new dress yet, or would it not last a little longer with judicious patching?" Was it fair to more careful mothers, who did not neglect the 'stitch in time,' that Mrs. should continually be getting grants of new clothes to replace those worn out before their time by her careless children? Such points as these only seem trivial to those who forget that equally 'trivial' disputes have repeatedly wrecked Governments.

When it became evident that the increasing demands upon the store would shortly make it bankrupt a system of budgeting in advance was instituted. Under this scheme each family was required to apprise the storekeeper what amount of clothing represented the minimum it could manage with during the next six months — a definite number of yards of material per man, woman, and child (the latter according to age) being laid down as the maximum. But even this system did not work smoothly for the stuff which would make four suits per puny child could barely be stretched to make three for a more substantially built youngster of the same age. Again, some children were 'harder upon' their clothing than others, and the authorities had to decide between issuing a supplementary allowance or letting them go naked. In the end, the supplementary clothing allowance caused so much dissension that a return to the old plan of fixed monthly credits was found necessary.

This clothing question was only one of a dozen causes of bickering which sprang up, when it became evident that hardship was not merely an initial difficulty, but seemed likely to remain a permanent feature of Cosme life. Newcomers in particular were affected by the poverty of the food supply. During the year 1899, when there were about 100 souls at

Cosme, the total edible stores consumed, exclusive of fruit and garden vegetables, were as follows: corn meal, 13 tons; mandioca, 33 tons; sweet potatoes, 25 tons; pumpkins, 3 tons; beans, 11 tons; treacle, 5 tons; sugar, 12 cwt. ; coffee, 11 cwt. ; tobacco, 41 cwt. ; beef, 81 cwt. ; bacon and ham, 14 cwt. ; pork, 8 cwt. ; lard, 2 cwt. ; fowls, 128; eggs, 10,000; milk, 907 gals.; game (including deer, agouti, armadillo, fish, etc.), about 10 cwt. Though in the aggregate this list looks quite imposing, a little calculation shows that the average daily allowance of non-vegetarian food was less than one-third of an egg and 5 ounces of meat per person.

Even such a meagre diet was only made possible by raising loans upon all the colony's movable possessions. The Administration was compelled to resort to the plan of mortgaging all vendible resources in spite of the fact that, as at New Australia, they were surrounded on all sides by readily saleable timber.

The most pressing problem confronting Cosme was still the need for importing (a) single women, to become the wives of Cosme bachelors, and thus tie them to the colony, and (b) married couples. But, owing to the fiasco in which Lane's campaign had ended, no more assisted passages could be expected from the Government for the present. Moreover the authorities in Asuncion were tired of hearing the grievances of stranded British subjects, so, for the future, it was laid down that would-be Cosmans must not only bear their own expenses but also deposit a sufficient sum with the Cosmo chairman to take them home again should they be dissatisfied. In the case of single women there was no such provision, however, as the following extraordinary regulation shows:

"Single women to pay their own passage to Asuncion but will

not be required to make any deposit or payment to the colony and will have passages to Buenos Aires paid by the colony should mutual trial not result in full membership; the colony may terminate the mutual trial of a single woman at any time and will provide such passage upon doing so; but passages will not be so provided for any single woman who may herself terminate mutual trial before the completion of three months residence."

Any man who could deliberately contemplate the stranding of unprotected English women in Buenos Aires, must be singularly ignorant of the deplorable conditions existing in that city. Possibly the framers of that regulation foresaw that most women would prefer to accept a Cosme suitor, however ineligible, and submit with docility to the miseries inseparable from Communism, rather than face the risks of far worse degradation in the Argentine capital. The reason given for exporting women ineligible for membership, to Buenos Aires was that there "employment at English wages can be got in the numerous English families." What must become of women, who were not lucky enough to fall at once into honourable employment, was not considered, apparently. William Lane was certainly nodding when he gave assent to such a regulation. It was not, in fact, surprising if Lane's old grip of affairs were beginning to relax. It was just six years since he had left Australia, at the head of a band of enthusiasts, "to teach the world a lesson," and during that period he had faced sufficient crushing disappointments to break the heart of any man. Latterly, moreover, he had lost the allegiance of some of his closest friends and supporters, and a large proportion of his flock were later recruits of a much lower intellectual order, many of whom were unmistakably opposed to him personally. Even his best friends were bound to admit that his expensive English campaign, which was to have achieved so much, had done the place a great deal more harm than good, and it is doubtful whether he would have been re-elected to the chairmanship, which he had hitherto monopolised (he had served during two periods of three years each), if he had stood for it. However, he did not stand. It was officially stated that: "In notifying his intention not to accept any nomination for further office-bearing, the retiring chairman, W, Lane, said that 'apart from health reasons which alone were more than sufficient,' he wished to become entirely free to propagandize."

By the popular vote William Lane's mantle fell upon his brother, John, who had hitherto acted as schoolmaster.

It would have been interesting to observe how 'King Billy' settled down to the arduous duties of a non-official — as a member of the 'hoeing gang,' for instance. Since the new chairman and his executive committee of three began very soon to transgress against William Lane's root principle, 'the non-employment of outside labour', it would have been illuminating to watch William's attitude towards them. Had he remained, would he have been expelled for contumacy, one wonders ? It is impossible to say, for shortly after the expiry of his second term of office William Lane shook the red earth of Paraguay from his boots, and went back to Australia, where he took over the editorship of the Sydney Worker, From that time the original apostle of Cosmeism disappeared for ever from the ken of Cosmans.

It is often asserted that William Lane 'deserted' Cosme when he forsook the place in 1899. But in this connection it should be remembered that, so long as he remained there, he was powerless to assist his wretched brethren financially, whereas by earning his living in the outside world he was able to remit from his earnings a 'loan' for the benefit of those who remained at Cosme. This non-Interest-bearing 'loan' of £211. 4s., which he must have known was unlikely to be repaid, figured first in the Cosme balance-sheet for May 1900.

John Lane's promotion to the chairmanship was marked by sundry alterations in the regulations (including reduction of the deposit made by trial members to £5 per adult) of which the principal was that relating to the employment of native labour. It was a fundamental principle of Cosmeism that the wages system was utterly wicked nevertheless the accursed thing found its way into Cosme twelve months after William Lane's departure. It began, of course, as a temporary expedient, but was found so convenient that principles went hang and the Cosmans as a body became employers of labour, battening upon the 'surplus value' of the natives' work in the forest and in the sugar-cane field.

"At a committee held on September 4th (1900)," says the official journal, "the chairman reported that unless otherwise instructed by the committee he intended advising the executive to have steps taken for the immediate felling of two acres of monte by native labour, in order to provide firewood to finish the season's crushing. It was pointed out that the work could not be done by colony labour without stoppage of crushing and planting; and as the results of the crushing were relied on to meet the financial obligations of the colony, such stoppages was altogether undesirable. The objections to the proposals were: the having natives working on the colony, and also to any hiring of labour. The voting on the committee resulted in a tie. The chairman refrained from using his casting vote, and, with the approval of the committee, left the matter over for decision by general meeting."

It is interesting to note that Alexander Dick, a member of the committee, resigned membership on September 4th, and subsequently left Cosme together with his three brothers and his mother, who had been organised in Glasgow in 1897. This did not affect the chairman's plans, however, for "At a special general meeting held on September 12th, it was resolved by 15 votes to 5 that the management be empowered to employ native labour to procure firewood in the present emergency."

Following this decision another committeeman, John Delugar, resigned on September 17th, but the loss of a few members was more than compensated for by the gain from the exploitation of native labour. In the year 1899, when the colonists did their own work, the sums received for sales of produce totalled £2,366; in 1901, the year following the new regulations, the receipts had leaped to £99,898; from May1st, 1903, to May 1st, 1904, they came to £920,658.

Of course the Cosmans tried to prove to themselves and to the outside world that they did not transgress the Socialist creed by employing native labour at such low wages (sixpence per day) that a handsome profit could be derived from their energies. But nobody was hoodwinked. From across the ocean came a letter which reproachfully stated that:
"Cosme is turning its back on its principles. . . . The colonists had fled from participation in the horrors of wage-slavery, sweating, exploitation of human labour by capitalists, etc., and now in far-off Paraguay they were introducing the evil system."

The Cosmans' defence to this just indictment is an amazing document:
"While recognising the evils of commercialism to such an extent as to feel it incumbent on us to live with each other in brotherhood, and not to work for each other for wages, or lend to each other for interest, or take rent from each other for land

or houses, but to care for and work for and share with each other in fellowship, we have never made any pretence of being guided in our business relations with outside non-co-operators by any other than business principles."

The writer of that statement had strayed very far indeed from the teaching of William Lane's gospel. Nevertheless, from the organising point of view, the distinction drawn between those within and those without the fold was a brilliantly conceived notion. When William Lane went recruiting he had nothing to offer but a share in the common poverty; how much more successful might a man be who could hold out the prospect of exploiting Cosme's resources by the labour of others for the Cosmans' benefit? Finding John Lane possessed of such a commonsense point of view the Paraguayan Government once more went to great expense to assist the Cosme Colony, when, in May, 1901, John Lane decided to try his fortune as an organiser, the emigration authorities paid his return fare round the world, and agreed to restore the original arrangement by which they paid the expenses of would-be Cosmans from Monte Video to the colony. At the same time the Cosme Monthly blossomed forth on greatly improved paper with an attractive illustration in each number, and a still more attractive balance sheet, exhibiting an excess of assets over liabilities amounting to £179,485.

As the population at the time consisted of only 26 men (four absent), 17 women, and 51 children, it would appear that, with such an ample balance, they could all have lived in clover, but as a matter of fact the Cosmans were enduring extraordinary hardships. The meat allowance had been suspended, and they were living entirely on a vegeterian diet, with the exception of a small allowance of semi-liquid lard, which was served out occasionally. As they pulled their belts tight to suppress the gnawing of hunger, how some of the men envied lucky John Lane his, delightful eighteen months' excursion in civilised England and Australia.

It was John Lane's intention to send a large number of recruits to Cosme in time for the 1902 sugar season, but in this he was disappointed. To his surprise, conditions had altered remarkably in Australia during the last nine years. He accounted to his impatient fellow-Cosmans for the slow progress he was making by explaining that "(1) The old unionism of the bush has gone back. (2) The old Socialistic idea has become much less prevalent. In fact it is only occasionally in these parts you drop across a Socialist. (3) There is a decided growth in the Imperialistic idea. In the old days there was very little of this. One part of the world was pretty near as good as another. There is a greater desire than heretofore to be under the British. (4) Drought has made it extremely difficult for men to raise the necessary funds to proceed to Cosme."

He might have added as a fifth reason that he did not, fortunately, possess his brother's magnetic personality. Nevertheless he contrived to send a certain number of recruits to Cosme before his own return in December, 1902. The newcomers, however, proved no better able to settle down happily with the 'old-timers' than William Lane's recruits.

In July, 1901, when John Lane sailed upon his organising campaign, the population of Cosme was 26 men, 16 women, 46 children. Total 88. By June, 1904, it had been reduced to 22 men, 11 women, and 36 children. Total 69.

As before, a dismissal, "for persistent defiance of Colony authority and regulations," and subsequent secessions of 'old-timers,' were largely responsible for the decrease (the expelled man was a member of six years' standing, who is was alleged "during the last four years had shown Anarchistic tendencies, and had throughout failed to work in harmony with those entrusted with the direction of the colony industries, while latterly his attitude had become increasingly and more openly antagonistic"). Out of the fifteen trial members, who were on the rolls in 1903, only four remained in 1904. The eleven who left were thus accounted for: "One had his membership terminated by the committee; one was notified that there was little chance of his being accepted as a full member, and he consequently took the first opportunity of going; one left because of disagreement with the colony regulation requiring full members to contribute their capital as a free gift to the colony; six left on account of dissatisfaction with or unfittedness for the conditions of the colony; two resigned owing to reasons other than dissatisfaction with the colony."

Thus John Lane's organising campaign proved as lamentable a failure as his brother's. In May, 1904, he was replaced by a new chairman, and next month the publication of the Cosine Monthly ceased.

At that date the colony's cash liabilities amounted to £31, against cash in hand £623. It is true that the two colonists who acted as auditors cheerfully set a value on the land, improvements, etc., of over £200,000, but they ignored the fact that the conditions attached to the grant of territory (the settlement of 72 families) had by no means been complied with. Something of the changed spirit of the place peeps out in the snarling tone of the final manifesto— so different from those penned by William Lane.

"Many people come here overloaded with cut and dry ideals" the writer complains. "This colony is not, and never has been, in anything like the full, usual, acceptance of the word, a Communistic one. We share equally the results of our common labour; not unequally. If one man's wants are greater than another's he has got to curb them. Here, as elsewhere, a man has got to make and win his own friendships. They aren't ready made for him. . . . The daily direction of common affairs is governed by officials elected yearly, whose instructions have got to be obeyed whether one agrees or differs from them...We employ native labour outside the village, mainly to develop our timber industry. We trust this necessity will not be continuous, but this is by the way, the point is, that we do at present, and will in all probability for some time to come, so employ for profit such labour."

Many secessions from Cosme were directly caused by the admission of natives to the place; several fathers of families withdrew ostensibly for other reasons, but really because they feared admixture with the Paraguayans. Among such were the Gilmores. When she reached Australia Mrs. Gilmore stated that there were people remaining at Cosme, with no intention of leaving it, who expressed their conviction that the children of some of those then resident would marry natives.

"Up to the time we left," she said in the Sydney Telegraph, "generally speaking, one might say, there had been no intercourse with natives... Speaking particularly as to certain cases, there had... That is what the colony has to look to."

The record of perpetual secessions, appearing in the Cosme Monthly had proved so poor an advertisement of the settlement in the past that it was perhaps a wise plan for the Cosmans to cease publication and keep domestic squabbles to themselves in future. Moreover, those who in the past possessed no vote, and were obliged to keep their actual beliefs to themselves, were now 'old-timers' with power to alter the Constitution, if they chose, as they thought fit. If they should come to any such decision there was no need to apprise the whole world of their intentions. After the departure of Leek, John Lane, and other original stalwarts, there was no longer any strong party with deep convictions on the subject of Cosmeism. Burdened with debt on the sugar-cane crushing plant, and other machinery which they had bought out of borrowed money, and sick of living lives of drudgery amidst surroundings no better than those of the natives, many of the Cosmans only stayed on in the hope of securing a share of the spoil when, if ever, the Government offered to pay off the bank mortgages on condition that Cosme should abandon its crippling principles.

CHAPTER XIX.

A BLACK TIME AT NEW AUSTRALIA.

To return now to New Australia, it has been shown that the affairs of the colonists at that settlement had got into a deplorable muddle. Yet, under any other system of living than the Socialist regime, they might yet have retrieved their position, for, as Mr. Peel remarked:

"in spite of their difficulties it must be recollected that they are in possession of 350,000 acres of the very finest land in Paraguay, with pasturage sufficient to keep) at least 70,000 head of cattle. . . . Buying cattle for purposes of fattening should yield in Paraguay a profit of at least 20 to 30 per cent., and the Association on starting expected that it would not be long before they were doing a good trade. They bought 2500 head and put up about eight miles of wire fencing, but owing to the causes mentioned this number has been already considerably reduced. ... In addition, they have got about 90 cows, 170 horses, and a large number of pigs and poultry. They have cleared about 70 acres of woodland .... and cultivated about 213 acres. . . . They have large forests of valuable timber, but no sawmills; they are engaged at this moment in making bricks to start a tannery, but the work is proceeding slowly for want of proper appliances, at a time too when they ought to be engaged in erecting houses in the place of the uncomfortable barns and sheds of mud and thatch in which they are at present living and even these are not put up in a sufficient number to shelter all the colonists, a few of whom at present are sleeping under tents. . . . They have started a band which plays every evening, and one of the first steps they will take as soon as their funds will permit, will be to build a hall for the purpose of lectures, and concerts, as well as dancing."

Any wild-cat scheme was good enough for New Australia to waste its energies upon, at a time when those energies were so paralysed that the place was not even self-supporting to the extent of growing a sufficient food supply for home use. Compare the 70 acres of forest land cleared at New Australia, in one year, by 250 persons, with the achievement of a single Frenchman on an individualistic colony in another part of Paraguay.

"At a short distance from the station," reported Mr. Findlay, after visiting Gonzalez, "we turned into a narrow 'picada' or lane cut through the virgin forest. Similar roads are cut parallel to each other at equal distances. On each side of the road at intervals were clearings planted with maize and mandioca. The first of these we visited, evidently the 'show' clearing, belonging to a Frenchman. This man had cleared a space of about 10 acres in 13 months.

"When we looked at the dense forest of hardwood trees, towering above a tangled mass of creepers and undergrowth, it seemed almost incredible that so much could have been accomplished by a single man (by no means a Hercules), whose principal instruments had been an axe and a box of matches. The little rancho was surrounded by maize, mandioca, mani (pea-nut), tobacco, beans, sugar-cane, alfalfa, melons, and every sort of vegetable. Some wheat had been grown, but was of poor quality, perhaps owing to bad seed. The colonist showed us a little hollow which he had converted into a miniature paddy-field, and the rice was coming up luxuriantly. What we actually saw growing represented a small fortune for this hard-working Frenchman,"

From this it would appear that one Frenchman working for himself is worth, as a colonist, some thirty-five Australians labouring for each other! (Though, as it will presently appear, the latter were easily able to outstrip all competitors when the energy-destroying regime of Socialism was abolished.) While the Frenchman plied his axe with a light heart in the forest, lived luxuriously, and rapidly piled up a comfortable competency, the Australians sank day by day into lower depths of misery and degradation.

It was a black time indeed at New Australia, but the natural phenomenon that the darkest hour immediately precedes the dawn, applied forcibly in their case. Now that there was no longer anything to be gained by Socialism, even the drones were willing to suspend it. By a vote of the majority it was decided that the Constitution should be altered; henceforth every man would be entitled to dispose as he pleased of the fruit of his own labour, and a new incentive was given to industry.

According to the Socialist creed this was a retrograde step that the New Australians were taking. There were one or two indeed who gloomily quoted Mr. Blatchford's dictum :
"With regard to the claim that men should be left free to fight each for his own hand — is that civilisation or anarchy? And will it result in peace or in war, in prosperity or in disaster? Not civilisation, but savagery; not Christianity, but cannibalism is the spirit of this doctrine of selfishness and folly... Is not love stronger than hate? And will not a society founded on love and justice certainly flourish, as the society founded on hate and strife will certainly perish?"

But to those pessimists others replied that neither love nor justice, nor prosperity, nor civilisation, but the reverse had been found under Socialism. In fact, in every particular the claims of the theorists had been falsified. The great majority of the New Australians hailed the final dethronement of Socialism as the dawn of a new and brighter day.

It was once said in, all reverence, by a famous newspaper editor that the Bible, with its terse, expressive, concentrated style, would remain for all time as an example of first-rate journalism. Certainly it would be hard to pen a paragraph more vividly describing the pass to which things had come, at New Australia, than Isaiah iii, 5;
"And the people shall be oppressed, every one by another, and every one by his neighbour. The child shall behave himself proudly against the ancient, and the base against the honourable."

Freedom of action was denied to all, the smallest details of each one's daily life were jealously spied upon by some other, and the degrading atmosphere of mistrust, which turned every man against his neighbour, was exploited by the base of their own ends.

A blight seemed to descend upon everything managed by the community, and the children proved no exception to the rule. Deliberately cut off from the softening influences of religion, and brought up to ignore all distinctions of age or sex it was natural for them to seek always their own pleasure and ride rough-shod over the old and infirm. Untaught and unrestrained, the neglected children seemed doomed to suffer all their lives for the follies of their parents. This was perhaps the saddest aspect of the New Australia fiasco.

As soon as the resolution, abolishing Socialism, was carried, Frederick Kidd, under whose sane and practical administration the change was brought about, set off to Asuncion to interview the Government, whom he found sympathetically disposed and prepared to do all in their power to assist the colonists. Withdrawing the original grant of territory, the President confirmed them in possession of the twenty-five square miles on which they were actually settled, and approved a scheme whereby every man was entitled to select for himself an allotment of sixty squares of agricultural ground, for which he would be given title deeds when he had built a house and complied with the usual conditions. The right of grazing over the grass lands was reserved in common for all, so that it was possible for every individual colonist to become a big cattle farmer if he could find the necessary capital. This fact created fresh ambition in the heart of every family, and there was a general exodus of able-bodied men to the railway works at Sapucay, to Asuncion, Rosario, or Buenos Aires — anywhere where good wages could be earned by a man willing to work his fingers to the bone.

One colonist, who now owns many hundred head of cattle, worked as a butcher in an Argentine meat works, where wages are high, living on the odd halfpence of his pay and remitting the balance to his wife, to be carefully invested in lean cattle, for which a ready market could be found when fattened. The Administrator himself looked for work as a bootmaker's assistant in Asuncion (he had once had a prosperous business of his own), but, to his delight, a leather merchant set him up with a stock of leather and even became responsible to a third party for the value of the necessary tools. Being a good workman, he soon made headway and became a cattle owner also though it was principally on his trade that he relied for a living. The story of other colonists was similar. One and all found salvation in the 'iron law of wages,' and discovered for themselves that Capital is the indispensable ally and friend, and not the enemy, of

Labour. The legitimate ambition of each one was to become himself a capitalist, for 'Capital is the result of Labour and Abstinence.'

There is a sentence in Levy's 'Outcome of Individualism' which well sums up the conditions at New Australia:
"A brief but brilliant span of existence may be attained by a Socialistic State living on the capital of its predecessors; but it soon runs through this capital and goes out like a spent squib and leaves a nasty smell."
The nasty smell at New Australia took the form of rancour and bitterness of spirit, so that many families were not on speaking terms with their nearest neighbour — not that anyone had time or inclination in those terrible days for sociabilities. Women, whose husbands were away earning wages, worked hard in the cornfields for themselves and for their children. The sternest Individualism now prevailed, for, when all were on the verge of starvation, no man would share his children's bread with the work-shirkers. There was no longer any talk of an eight hour day, or of Trade Union regulations as to what particular task a given individual might perform. From sunrise to sunset men, women, and even children worked at whatever task came first to hand, unheeding the rays of the tropical sun. Even the coming of night did not see the cessation of their labours when the moon's bright light illuminated the cornfields. In an incredibly short space of time houses shot up, surrounded by well-tilled kitchen gardens, carefully fenced in to keep men or brutes from damaging the crops, and very soon the grass lands were once more dotted with cattle — cheap, sorry beasts some of them, but precious beyond all reckoning for the sake of the regained joy of ownership which they personified. It was not long, moreover, before the self-banished fathers and husbands were able to return with money in their pockets and restored hopefulness.

Some used the money thus earned to convey themselves and their dear ones back to Australia, others determined to make the most of the country's natural advantage and to combine the rearing of cattle with lumbering operations or store-keeping. On these lines rapid progress was made, and, within a few years, many of the 130 colonists who remained at New Australia possessed from 100 to 600 head of cattle and horses, to say nothing of pigs, poultry, etc., and in addition grew a great deal of fruit, vegetables, and maize (for the last of which, as also for all kinds of live-stock there was always a good market).

It must not be imagined, of course, that every colonist was equally successful. Nature does not discount the intelligent industry of the energetic, or supplement the efforts of the idle, incompetent, or stupid, in order to level things down "without regard to sex, age, office, or physical or mental capacity." But even the laziest were compelled by necessity to do infinitely more for themselves than they ever did under Socialism, while the industrious were encouraged by that self-interest which is so essential to progress, by means of forethought, thrift, and diligence, to put by for their old age and lay the foundations of prosperity for their children.

It would be pleasant to record that the instant change for the better at New Australia was spiritual as well as physical. But unfortunately that was not so — for many years at least. The hatreds which had sprung up during the period of Socialist rule left deep feuds which it took a long time to heal, and the mutual jealousies were so bitter that even the children, who lived at the villages of Los Amigos, or Loma Rugua, were hardly on speaking terms with those of Las Ovejas or Tuyu. Worse than that, such bitterness had arisen in some cases between members of the same family that father and son who lived on adjacent blocks forbade one another to cross the dividing fence. Moreover everyone's energies were now concentrated to such an extent upon the anxious desire to repair the ruin of their fortunes that nobody worried about such a matter as the need for educating the children. In consequence lads and lasses grew up in total ignorance, except for those few who attended a native school and acquired Indian habits of thought together with the Guarani tongue.

Nor was such a state of things wholly accidental, for there were loud-voiced men upon the colony who claimed that education was in itself an evil, while many held as the fundamental article of their belief that religion was the curse of the world. Nevertheless, when Bishop Every (Anglican Bishop in the Argentine) took a long and wearisome journey for the purpose of visiting the colonists, some of them approached him privately and begged him to send a schoolmaster to New Australia. The Bishop stated the case in England, and a young Cambridge man (who was ordered abroad for the benefit of his health) volunteered to go out at his own expense and do what he could for the children. It will not be without interest, perhaps, to a certain number of readers, to follow the youthful pedagogue to Paraguay and see how he fared at New Australia.

CHAPTER XX.

NEW AUSTRALIA AND COSME TO-DAY.

It was the month of March, 1904, when the Schoolmaster arrived at New Australia. By correspondence it had been arranged that he should board with the T family, at La Novia. His first view of this, one of the earliest village settlements, was extremely depressing. Situated on a clearing just within the forest, it still consisted of the original, roughly-built mud huts, which the pioneers had thrown up nearly eleven years before. In all there were five half-ruined houses, in such bad condition that it was necessary to re-dress the walls with thick coatings of mud several times a year to keep them from tumbling down. Interesting illustration of the value of work done 'by all for all' was forthcoming on close examination of the material used in the construction of some of these houses. Much of the wood used was soft and unsuitable for the work, but easier to handle than the hard woods. The floors were still of mud or ant-bed, although good timber was abundant, and the rough walls of red 'pug' were not even smoothed inside. Though so many years had passed since they were first built, some of them were still without any verandah to keep the torrential rains from washing away the walls. Neither fire place nor windows were provided (pivoted wooden shutters served to exclude the cold) and the draught-admitting gaps, between roof and walls, made it impossible to keep a lamp alight when the wind blew.

The house in which it was arranged that the Schoolmaster should board contained three rooms, and a low lean-to in which the colonist's three sons slept. Originally it had consisted of two rooms separated by a 'galpone' (a covered space open on two sides), but the latter had been boarded in with pieces of packing case, etc., to form a living room. The kitchen was a separate outbuilding. As if the house were not sufficiently overcrowded the T children kept an amazing number of pets, which wandered in and out of the house as they chose. In addition to the dogs, of which four lived principally indoors, there were a tame owl, several pigs, which had to be forcibly ejected at meal times, and a miscellaneous collection of fowls, wandering where they pleased and even roosting in the bedrooms. The average Irish hut would compare more than favourably with the T home-stead.

It must not be supposed, however, that all the homes at New Australia were of this type. After the abolition of Socialism it became worthwhile for any individual who prized hygiene and comfort to erect better accommodation for his family. After leaving La Novia, the next village settlement, reached by a rough track cut through the forest, was Tuyu Rugua, a big clearing on the edge of the open plain, well enclosed with strong fencing, with two very large paddocks stretching down into the low-lying land towards the river. At the time of the disruption, when each colonist chose his favourite site on which to settle and build, the K contingent, consisting of old Mr. K — the father of the colony — and his five sons, took up their allotments all together, each allotment consisting partly of camp and partly of monte, in the proportion settled by the rules governing New Australia. Thus they monopolised all the frontage to the camp at that point, and no room was left for anyone else to settle there. In consequence the Ks jointly possessed quite a large domain, which they had turned into a valuable property by assiduous labour. Their well-built homes were a standing reproach to those lazy individuals who were still content to live in squalor.

In the first house lived old Mr. and Mrs. K with two adult sons. In addition to owning cattle, and engaging in agriculture they kept a store and traded in timber with the merchants of Villa Rica and Caballero. Through the slip-rails was the home of Alf. K , an industrious cattle farmer.

The walls of his house, built after the 'split' by himself, almost unaided, were fortified by stout planks of cedar and hard-wood, felled in the forest and sawn with infinite labour. A double verandah protected the outside walls, and the interior, with its cooking-range, its smooth walls artistically tinted, its serviceable furniture and well-constructed floor was as comfortable as an English villa. The well-dressed children played happily upon the big lawn surrounding the house and took a keen interest in their flower garden. The builder of this happy home who, by sheer hard work, had regained prosperity, offered the Schoolmaster a warm welcome and promised to send his three children for tuition.

So the Schoolmaster rode on, across open camp, through bog and forest visiting every house in this scattered community, and hearing many amazing theories of life. "You think we're a lot of cranks," said one man. "Well, of course we are, or we shouldn't be here. We came to Paraguay to get away from convention, and be as cranky as we please. If you're a crank too we're delighted to welcome you, but if you are a missionary, whose object is to teach our children all the old conventional lies, that we have run away from, you will find the colony an unhealthy place to live in."

This man's remark was a frank statement of the general feeling. The New Australians had set out to teach the world a lesson; and many of them resented the suggestion that an outsider could instruct them or their children in anything. On the whole, however, the Schoolmaster was well received, chiefly perhaps because he was a good listener and took an interest in each rival scheme propounded for the readjustment of the universe.

That night the Schoolmaster slept at a tiny cabin on the extreme boundary of the colony, and next morning started on his return trip by a different route, so as to take in Loma Rugua and Los Amigos, thus making a complete circuit of New Australia. Notwithstanding the conviction expressed by many colonists that he would not remain with them more than a few weeks, the Schoolmaster felt quite hopeful, and asked the Administrator to call a general meeting for the purpose of discussing plans for the establishment of a school. Messages were sent accordingly to all the stores, fixing a date for the meeting, and the Schoolmaster employed a couple of 'handy-men' to knock together some rough forms and desks.

On the day appointed for the general meeting every colonist who could find a horse rode over to Las Ovejas. The Schoolmaster, though already assured of considerable support from the Los Amigos, La Novia, and Tuyu Rugua contingents, anticipated a stormy scene, and in this he was not disappointed. Most of the assembled citizens proved to be stern-browed, bearded men, with faces tanned to the colour of mahogany from constant exposure; they were dressed in the usual costume — riding boots, baggy trousers, and rough shirt, loose at the neck — and most carried revolvers and sheath knives; some had long machetes secured to their saddles, while one or two even carried rifles.

It looked more like a Council of War than a peaceful assembly; but everyone's intentions were harmless enough. It is the usual thing to wear revolver and sheath knife on all occasions in the Paraguayan bush country, and a machete is constantly required, in riding through narrow forest tracks, to cut away any vines and tangled scrub which impede the way. Those with guns or rifles were the sportsmen of the community, who hoped to carry home venison or wild game to the family larder.

As this was the first occasion on which many of the men had met for five years, or more, it was only to be expected that old, half-forgotten feuds should be revived. Certain rival politicians, who had argued against each other in the early days of the colony, took the opportunity to display again the rancour of party feeling. It was sufficient for any one man to make a proposal to produce a storm of objections from old foemen on the instant. In fact, after a time, there were almost as many counsels as there were people present — many insisting that a 'gentleman' from England, 'who had never done a fair day's work in his life,' had no right at New Australia at all, and, least of all, the right to set up a school in which to teach Capitalistic notions to the rising generation.

Nevertheless, when the Schoolmaster rose to speak he was given a fair hearing. Taking his cue from their own profession of equality, he claimed that he had as much right as any other person to settle at New Australia. Next, he argued that it would be an unwarrantable interference with private liberty if the majority refused to allow any settler who chose to open a school if he were so disposed, or if any other settlers were prohibited from sending their children to school if they so desired. Though there were some who hotly contested the claim (a few on the ground that 'book-learning' was in itself an evil), its justice was finally admitted, and the Schoolmaster gained his first point, though only on condition that religious instruction should be excluded from the curriculum. So much conceded, the Schoolmaster then entered upon a fresh argument, in favour of holding a Sunday School, quite independent of the Day School, which at once aroused a storm of opposition.

It was hardly surprising, considering that they honestly believed with Mr. Blatchford that the Christian religion was false and an obstacle to progress, that many desired to see it still excluded from New Australia. It was just at that time that Nunquam's popular assault upon religion: "God and my Neighbour" was published, and it nowhere met with a warmer welcome than at New Australia. It was only logical, therefore, for some convinced atheists to assert that they "would run the School-master off the Colony if he got trying to introduce religion." Nevertheless, the Schoolmaster secured a majority in favour of permitting him to hold Sunday School, after a long and exhausting debate, to which the Administrator contributed the commonsense remark that any parents who did not want their children taught religion could keep them away on Sundays.

Thus school teaching commenced at New Australia, and soon there were fifteen (shortly increased to twenty-six) children in attendance, many of whom had to ride or walk great distances to reach the school-house. Having spent their days hitherto in running wild upon the camps, or in the forest, as unaccustomed to discipline and restraint as the birds of the air, it was very difficult at first for the children to sit still in class, and the Schoolmaster had to resort to unaccustomed methods of teaching to retain their attention. It was singularly interesting to note the wonderfully rapid progress made by many of the hitherto untutored lads and lasses, who literally lapped up knowledge, with an avidity wholly unlike the indifference to learning displayed by most more happily circumstanced children. The deplorable state of disunion which had so long prevailed at New Australia was demonstrated by the fact that children from different parts of the settlement at first formed hostile cliques. Thus, the Los Amigos children had little in common with those from Tuyu, and it was very difficult to induce them to play together. All such artificial distinctions soon disappeared however, and it became evident that the school would have a powerful effect in the healing of old feuds.

The following true incident illustrates the distinctly primitive notions entertained by some of the children.

As the water in the school-house well was rather bad, the Schoolmaster was in the habit of sending one boy, or two girls, with a bucket to bring good cool water from a spring bubbling up just inside the forest. Whenever the Schoolmaster fetched this water himself it was particularly clear and bright, but when the children brought it was often quite muddy. One day the Schoolmaster had sent two girls to fill the bucket in the usual way, but started after them to show them how to draw it without stirring up the bottom. The mystery was explained when the Schoolmaster reached the monte and found, resting upon the empty bucket, a small heap of clothes, and the two girls having a glorious bathe in the spring. They were quite surprised when he remonstrated with them, "You mustn't bathe in my drinking water, you know," he told them. "That is very dirty. I don't like to drink water that you have bathed in." "Oh, but sir," they exclaimed together, "we don't use soap!"

Finding that his spring was the regular bathing place for those little girls, the Schoolmaster had a large pit dug beside it, and arranged that the over-flow from the spring should run into it, so that in future they might have their bathe, and he his water, without mutual interference. Within a short time the Schoolmaster added to his other duties a night-school, which a number of young men attended on three evenings a week with great earnestness. By way of a return for his services, they good-naturedly consented to attend Sunday school also, and, in a short time, it became a commonplace to hear them singing English hymns to the accompaniment of guitar or concertina when the day's work was done, not from any devotional motive, but because they knew no other English songs. Another result of the Sunday school was that children would take their hymn books home, and plague their parents to assist them in committing to memory next Sunday's hymns (since they could not yet read). In consequence, the mothers were re-familiarised with the old words they had themselves learned in their childhood's days in Australia or Great Britain. With little persuasion they began to drop in at Sunday school to hear the children singing, and so, imperceptibly almost, the proceedings changed to a regular Service, attended by adults as well as children. The arrival from England of a portable harmonium was signalised by the establishment of a regular choir night. Within a short time, in fact, Divine Service on Sunday became a favourite institution at New Australia, which people rode long distances to attend, bringing provision for an al fresco picnic under the school verandah or in the shade of an orange grove.

Quite apart from their religious significance, it would be hard to exaggerate the good effect upon the general tone of the colony of those weekly reunions, which worked wonders in the patching up of differences, and the renewing of old friendships. At the same time they promoted the growth of a healthy public opinion, which went a long way towards checking intemperance and other abuses that had become too common on the settlement. By a coincidence the admission of the Deity to New Australia synchronised with a remarkable improvement in material prosperity and general progress. Official proof of this fact may be found in the Report of the British Consul for Paraguay, for the year 1908. Under the heading 'New Australia,' Mr. Consul Griffith reports as follows:

"The following data are taken from an interesting report which has been furnished to me by the Manager of the colony, Mr. Kennedy. The colonists number 161:86 adults and 75 minors. They are, with few exceptions, all British subjects — Australians, English, Irish, and Scotch. The colony, which is agricultural and pastoral, is said to be prospering slowly but surely, but no marked progress can be expected until the means of communication are improved, as the lands are thirty miles distant from a railway or river, and, consequently, being unable to market their produce, the colonists confine their cultivation to the growing of food-stuffs, fruits, and vegetables for their own consumption. Cattle and horses do well on the grazing lands of the colony, and to these the colonists have, at present, to look for an income. Notwithstanding the lack of communication and consequent heavy cost of transport, a man with a family can cultivate tobacco with advantage. Maize, cassava, many varieties of beans, sweet potatoes, sugar-cane, bananas, oranges, and peaches are successfully cultivated, and experiments which have been made with the yerba tree appear to be giving good results. The colony possesses a well-equipped steam saw mill, five stores, a small petit grain distillery, and two cana (rum) stills."

Thus the stalwarts who remained after the collapse of William Lane's wild venture have made a gallant fight back to prosperity, and have disproved the allegation that it was the nature of the country, rather than the evils inseparable from Socialism, which caused the original failure. At the present day the prosperity of those who remain at New Australia colony is steadily increasing, and a number of the original Utopians who were repatriated have found their way back to Paraguay, to share in the great advantages which the settlement offers to Anglo-Saxons with agricultural experience. If, as seems probable, the new Trans-Paraguay railway, now in course of construction, passes close to New Australia the place is likely to experience a boom, and the settlement there of many hundreds of Australian families may yet become a reality. Already conditions are vastly different from what they were at the commencement of 1904. The children are now well cared for, in all respects, and compare well with those more happily circumstanced in England. At the present day, New Australia is neither a Utopian Eden nor a 'hell upon earth.' It is an average community of sane, sober, hard-working, self-respecting farmers, living at peace with one another and taking for their motto: 'What we have we hold!' Never again will they submit their fortunes to the ruinous rule of Socialism in any guise — whether it call itself 'Christian Socialism,' 'Atheistic Socialism,' or merely ''Co-operative Communism.'

As has been seen, Cosme for many years made no such progress. Till 1904 it endeavoured to keep itself afloat by the publication in its journal of far-fetched articles describing the happiness of its people, which induced other credulous souls to join them in the expectation of experiencing impossible bliss. Cheated by false hopes, these newcomers quickly fell into the growing quagmire of discontent and misery. Things became worse every year; the original glamour faded, and men's hearts hardened as they had done at New Australia. The feeling of bitterness against those who were sick and unable to work, and against widows, and people with large families parasitically dependent upon the exertions of the adult able-bodied, was the saddest feature of the place. It often happened that a man, who was seriously ill, would stagger to his work when he should have been lying up, for fear of the boycotting which came to be systematically practiced towards any who failed to do their allotted day's task. Rather than work for the benefit of 'all' any longer, many of the bachelors withdrew to Sapucay, and obtained employment at the engineering works of the Paraguay Central Railway.

Married men, with families of young children, remained tied to the spot, hopelessly striving to make headway against the dead-weight of debt — for everything was mortgaged — which bore them down.

Eventually, as at New Australia, the Government stepped in, withdrew the original grant, and divided the Cosme settlement up, on the usual colonisation terms, each family *being allotted so much agricultural and so much grazing land*. *"The Cosme Colony has now definitely thrown its dreams over-board,"* wrote a correspondent to an Australian journal. "For several years before it abandoned the original principles, it was an open secret (scarcely even concealed by the interested parties) that the few remaining members were held together only by the expectation of the final break-up, when the property would be divided, and the fewer that remained the greater individual share would accrue to each."
Thus, after wasting the best part of their lives in hopeless experiments, the Cosmans were given a new lease of life and they, too, began to make some progress towards prosperity. As at New Australia, a schoolmaster, appointed by Bishop Every, now instructs the children and holds religious services.

A game of Cricket at Cosme

CHAPTER XXI.

RELIGION— MORALITY— SUICIDE.

Continental Socialism is frankly Atheistic, but in English-speaking countries the existence of that curious hybrid, the Christian Socialist, obscures the issue and makes it appear to some that there is nothing necessarily antagonistic between Socialism and Christianity. The whole question is too wide a one to be thrashed out here, though the reader may be reminded of Professor Flint's observation that that portion of the Christian Socialists teaching which is definitely Christian is not Socialistic, while that portion which is definitely Socialistic is not Christian. An ardent Christian and Social Reformer, carried away by admiration for some portion of the Socialist programme which coincides with his own views on Social reform, is frequently described by himself as a Christian Socialist, although he would repudiate with horror the views of any eminent Socialist on the subject of Christianity.

The logical attitude of the genuine Socialist toward Christian Socialism is well shown in the following reference: '"Socialism is the natural enemy of religion. A Christian Socialist is an Anti-Socialist. No man can consistently be both a Christian and a Socialist."

The fundamental difference between Socialism and Christianity has been well summed up in 'Ethics of Socialism,' by Mr. Belfort Bax:
"According to Christianity regeneration must come from within. The ethics and religion of modern Socialism, on the contrary, look for regeneration from without, from material conditions

and a higher social life."
Again, in his 'Religion of Socialism,' the same writer explains:
"In what sense Socialism is not religious will be now clear. It
utterly despises the other world with all its stage properties —
that is, the present objects of religion."

Since this work is intended for general circulation he writer
refrains from quoting any of the more crudely offensive
references to Christianity in which leading Socialists delight.

As Mr. Robert Blatchford ('Nunquam' of the Clarion), author of
'Merrie England', is the Socialist writer with most influence and
the widest circulation, the adult English reader, whose own
faith is firmly implanted, and who wishes to understand the
Socialist attitude towards religion, cannot do better than
procure his book, 'God and my Neighbour,' which has run
through fourteen editions. That book concludes with the words,
"Let the Holy have their Heaven. I am a man and an Infidel...
Christianity is not true."

Lest it should be argued that it is a mere coincidence that Mr.
Blatchford, the Socialist, should also be an opponent of religion,
it is worth while quoting Mr. Blatchford's own reason for "going
out of his way to attack religion.":
"In reply, I beg to state (1) that I have not 'gone out of my way'
to attack religion. It was because I found religion in my way that
I attacked it. (2) That I am working for Socialism when I attack a
religion which is hindering Socialism. (3) That we must pull
down before we can build up, and that I hope to do a little
building if only on the foundation."

It is because Socialists see that Socialism cannot finally triumph
until religion loses its hold upon the people that Socialist
Sunday schools have been established, to inculcate the class

war, in place of 'peace on earth, good-will among men, from infancy. Instead of hearing the gentle words of Him who said, 'Let the little ones come unto Me and forbid them not,' the tiny mites who attend those places are taught to lisp:

Who is from aye a slave
To all the tyrant brood?
Who oft for them must fight?
And for them shed his blood? —

O folk I has thou not yet perceived,
'Tis thou that ever art deceived
Awake, ye men who toil
Up, Proletariat!
Awake ye men, ye men who toil
Up, Proletariat

Modern Socialists have realised that the nullification of religious belief can be brought about much more easily by preserving a semblance to the outward forms of religion than by suppressing Sunday observances altogether. If careless parents, who let their children attend such Sunday schools, feel any doubts, they are quite set at rest on hearing that the Bible is actually used in them. How it is used, and what importance is attached to its teaching, appears from the following extract from instructions for conducting Sunday schools:

22. Lessons for older children (aged 11 to 13)

(1) Stories from Greek mythology, such as the Siege of Troy, etc.
(2) Stories from some of Shakespeare's plays, such as The Tempest, etc.
(3) Stories from Tennyson, Browning, etc.
(4) Stories from the chief sacred literatures —

Bible, Talmud, 'Buddhist Birth stories,' etc., lives of Buddha,
Mohammed, Confucius, etc.
(5) Lives of the Saints, etc.
(6) Stories of Greeks and Romans, etc.
(7) 'Child's Socialist Reader,' etc.
(8) Systematic Moral lessons, etc.

23. The Senior Class should not have set moral lessons.

When a child has been taught that a jumble of stories from the
Classics, the Vedas, the Koran, etc., are of equal importance, in
a religious sense, with the Bible narrative, it is no more
probable that he will turn Christian when he reaches years of
discretion than that he will become a Mohammedan.

The establishment of a Socialist government in this country
would prepare the way for Anti-Christ in a single generation.
Some effects of the banishment of religion from a community
have been illustrated in the story of New Australia. One of the
most startling of the phenomena which mark the spread of
Socialism on the Continent is the increase of suicide, particularly
among young children and the aged.

In the light of history, however, this deplorable sign of the times
can hardly be considered surprising, for a materialist creed has
ever tended to the light holding of life.

Among the ancients, a high value was set on life by those who
maintained the immortality of the soul and vice versa. In
modern times, while suicide is regarded with abhorrence by
those who hold any religious belief, materialists advocate a
State-aided system of euthanasia for those who are weary of
living. Self-destruction was considered wholly permissible by
Zeno, that Stoic leader who foreshadowed modern Socialism in

his cosmopolitan 'Republic,' where money should not circulate, and where courts of justice, churches, and family life would have no place. His disciple, Seneca, for years before he died by his own hand, devoted much anxious thought to the 'way out.'

In precisely the same way, Paul Lafargue, son-in-law and disciple of Karl Marx, the founder of Modern Socialism, deliberately planned the date of his own extinction ten years in advance.

The celebrated author of *Le droit à la paresse* devoted himself with zeal, from the days of the Commune onwards, to the propagation of Socialism not only on the Continent but in England also. When he committed suicide (in November, 191 1) by means of prussic acid, hypodermically injected, he was suffering from no painful disease as his last testament shows.

"Sound in body and mind," he declared, "I am killing myself before ruthless old age, which has taken from me one by one the pleasures and joys of existence, and has deprived me of my physical and intellectual powers, paralyses my energy, and breaks my will and makes me a burden to myself and others.

"For many years I have pledged myself not to pass the threescore years and ten; I have fixed the time for my departure from life, and I have prepared the method of carrying out my resolution — a hypodermic injection of prussic acid.

"I die with the supreme joy of being absolutely certain that, in the near future, the cause to which I have devoted myself for forty-five years will triumph."

Nor was this an isolated case, due to some personal eccentricity of Lafargue, the chosen disciple of Karl Marx, for two of the latter's daughters, who were equally impregnated with the pure gospel of Socialism took their own lives. The first was Eleanor, wife of Dr. Edward Aveling, leading Socialist and lecturer in biology at London University; the second was Laura, wife of Paul Lafargue, who perished with him.

This is not the place to embark upon an elaborate examination of the ethics of suicide The writer wishes, however, to emphasise the fact, upon which medical authorities are agreed, that suicide does not necessarily imply insanity; the discovery that all mundane things are vanity, coupled with unbelief in extra-mundane compensations, may quite reasonably induce a sane, strong-minded Atheist to end his profitless existence from sheer boredom. If this be the case, it is to be expected that the revival of a purely pagan outlook on life will be accompanied by public approval of, and hasty resort to, the 'way out,' for the most trifling of reasons.

The tendency for suicide to associate itself with Socialism was illustrated in a remarkable manner at New Australia. When the Schoolmaster arrived there in 1904 he called upon A, one of the original settlers, a hard-working decent man, with a comfortable house, surrounded by much evidence of praiseworthy industry. A, who had married a Scottish woman — a, seceder from Cosme — was a man of considerable intelligence, an extreme Socialist, and an Atheist. He was universally liked, especially by the children, and was remarkably gentle in his manners. He was, in fact, quite the last man of whom one would expect any violent action. Yet, next time the Schoolmaster visited that house, it was in tragic cirumstances; A had killed his wife and taken his own life. How little that poor woman thought, when she left her home in Scotland, to experience the joys of Cosmeism, that this would be her fate!

Next, there was B, a man of education and the kindest and most generous disposition. In his case, fortunately, assistance came in time, and the Schoolmaster had the satisfaction of nursing him back to complete recovery.

C, was a personal friend of the Schoolmaster. An Englishman of sterling worth, a veteran who had fought many years before against the redskins in the Western States of North America. A bachelor and teetotaler, C was so devoted to children that the Schoolmaster employed him as caretaker and assistant at the Las Ovejas school, which he conducted single-handed during the rainy seasons, when the floods made it impossible for the Schoolmaster himself to get there, from La Novia, for a week or more at a time. When the Schoolmaster returned to England, towards the end of 1905, he continued to pay a small salary to C to carry on the school until someone else could take up the work. Sometime later he was inexpressibly shocked to learn that C had died, by his own hand, in tragic circumstances.

These cases, which all occurred within a period of eighteen months, among a population of less than ninety adults, while proving nothing, certainly lend colour to the theory of some intimate association between suicide and Socialism.

Since the honourable position of woman in the modern State is entirely due to the influence of religion upon conduct, accumulating through the ages, it is not surprising to find Socialists themselves admitting that the destruction of religion will be accompanied by the degradation of womankind. Although this subject has been touched upon in Chapter V, the following quotations from works by leading Socialists may be added :

"In the new moral world the irrational names of man and wife, parent and child, will be heard no more. All connection will be the result of affection . . . (woman) in her trial will be comforted and caressed by the whole community... the children will undoubtedly be the property of the whole community," — Robert Owen.

"Because we hold that Socialism will ultimately survive as the only tenable moral code, we are convinced that our present marriage custom and present marital law alike must soon collapse." — Professor Karl Pearson in 'Socialism and Sex.'

"Human beings must be in a position to act freely where their strongest impulse is concerned, as in the case of any other natural instinct... No one has to give an account of himself or herself, and no third person has the slightest right of intervention." — Herr Bebel in 'Woman.'

Evidence may be adduced to an indefinite extent to show that such ideas are not confined to an extreme set of writers in some one country. They are the common property of sober-minded, well-living, Socialist thinkers of all countries, at the present moment. Any reader who doubts the truth of this assertion, need only apply to any of the well-known Socialist organisations for a list of leaflets and works dealing with the subject. This is not a topic upon which the writer cares to dilate at any length in a work of this character. It may be stated however, that, small though the community was, illegitimacy was not unknown at 'New Australia.'

Such a statement may easily be met by an assertion that irreligion, suicide, and loose morals are by no means unusual phenomena in society as at present constituted. True, but whereas, at present, such evils are legislated against, and to a great extent kept under by the force of a strong public opinion, under a Socialistic regime they will be deliberately approved and fostered by the State. That is a distinction which makes all the difference. Those who have studied at close quarters the manners and customs of primitive races will see a close correspondence between their habits and the ideals of Socialism. It is difficult to resist the conclusion that State Socialism amounts to nothing less than a hideous form of State-enforced barbarism.

CHAPTER XXII.

CONCLUSION.

Although it is notoriously dangerous to prophesy, the progress which the New Australians commenced to make immediately Socialism was abandoned, irresistibly suggests the query: Supposing a similar attempt at colonisation had been made in Paraguay, by the same people, with equal capital, but on an Individualistic or simple co-operative basis, what would have been the result?

From personal observation on the spot, from careful discussions with those New Australian colonists who have snatched some measure of success from failure, and from the opinions expressed by other Englishmen who have prospered exceedingly in Paraguay, the writer has formed his own conclusion. It is his firm conviction that, if New Australia had been run on ordinary commercial lines, so that every individual was encouraged to labour by the knowledge that he, and his children, would enjoy the fruits of his industry, the venture would have proved an unqualified success. The landing in South America of a great body of sturdy Anglo-Saxon colonists might have done as much for that continent as the advent of the New Englanders did for North America. Paraguay would have awakened from its long stagnation and resumed its place as one of the most progressive of the sister Republics; the English bondholders and others, whose interests in Paraguay run into millions, would, among others, have reaped the benefit of its renewed prosperity.

By this, the twentieth year of New Australia's existence, the territory should have become a great centre of industry, dotted with prosperous towns, connected by railway with the Brazilian ports, as well as with Asuncion and the Argentine. These and much greater things could, and, in the writer's opinion would, have been achieved, had the New Australians not been burdened with the curse of Socialism. If, instead, patriotism had been the animating spirit of the New Australian movement, it thrills the imagination to project a vision of what might have been accomplished. But patriotism has nothing in common with Socialism.

Mismanagement, extravagance, favouritism, indolence, discontent, heathenism, these are the necessary accompaniments of Socialism; while industry, economy, thrift, independence, self-respect, and satisfaction are sterling qualities called forth by legitimate pride in individual ownership. Of this truism the plain story of New Australia serves as an excellent illustration.

William Lane set out to provide the world with an object lesson — and succeeded in doing so. But history shows that the world has rarely profited by object lessons. Nations, like individuals, usually insist on buying their own experience. From the rapid progress Socialism is making to-day, it seems probable that there are those now living who will see modern civilisation reduced to chaos by it. The sordid drama rehearsed, on a tiny stage, at New Australia and Cosme, may soon be played on a vast scale with the whole world for a theatre. When that day comes it will be tragedy indeed.

The End.

APPENDIX A: Political Platform

Political platform of the A. L. F. issued after THE COLLAPSE OF THE MARITIME STRIKE OF 1896.

"The general Council of the Australian Labour Federation recommends to its various districts the consideration of such political action as is demanded by the increasing intelligence of the age, and the desire for social justice which now moves the workers of the world.

Federated political action is a force, the potency of which, if rightly appreciated, is second only to federated social action. All forces must be availed of, if it is the purpose of the workers of Australia to root out those social wrongs which deprive the workers in other lands of all the happiness of living, and already show themselves in this so-called 'paradise' of the working-man.

This general Council is individually and collectively convinced, and believes, as the vast majority of thinking workers are coming to believe that social misery, poverty, vice, and enmity are the natural fruits of the industrial system as it exists to-day, denying to the workers the liberty to work and live except by permission of a class which is permitted to hold for its own advantage the means of production and distribution, without which none can live. And this general Council is further convinced, and believes, that by industrial re-organisation, as hereafter proposed, every man or woman would be insured work, every old person and young person and sick person would be insured comfort, and every child born into the State would be ensured full opportunity to

develop its brain and body as is possible in our civilisation, did we only cease to compete with one another.

'Therefore this general Council recommends and urges the unions and members of the Federation to authorise its executive to declare that the present industrial system, commonly called the competitive system, is destructive, pernicious, and altogether evil and must be replaced by a social system which will not leave it in the power of one man to take advantage of the necessities or disabilities of another, and which will provide for all the workers opportunities to avail themselves of the bounties of nature, and to partake fully of the fruits of civilisation, to receive the full benefit of their share of the common toil.

The Federation's political aims are stated thus:
1. The nationalisation of all sources of wealth and all means of production and exchanging wealth.

2. The conducting by the State authority of all production and all exchange.

3. The pensioning by the State authority of all child, aged, and invalid citizens.

4. The saving by the State authority of such proportion of the joint wealth-production as may be requisite for installing, maintaining, and increasing national capital.

5. The maintenance by the State authority from the joint wealth-production of all education and sanitary institutions.

6. The just division among all the citizens of the State of all wealth-production, less only that part retained for public and common requirements.

7. The re-organisation of society upon the above lines to be commenced at once, and pursued uninterruptedly until social justice is fully secured to each and every citizen. "

APPENDIX B: ARTICLES OF ASSOCIATION.

Chapter I. —Name, Object, Duration,

Art. I. The Name of the Company is 'The New Australia Co-operative Colonization Society,' founded to carry out the objects expressed in the following articles.

Art. II. The object of the Company is to acquire and pioneer the lands granted by the Paraguayan Government in the Departments of Ajos, Villa Rica, Mbocyaty, Caaguazu, and other lands that may be acquired beforehand, with the object of forming a Co-operative Colony.

Art. III. The Company will have its head office or seat in the colony Nueva Australia, Department of Ajos, Paraguay.

Art. IV. The duration of the Society remains fixed for twenty years, to count from the day on which these statutes are approved by the Superior Government. This term can be prolonged by a general meeting of shareholders whose members represent three-quarters of the total number of shares subscribed.

Art. V. The Society can cease before the limit of duration by a decision of a general meeting called for that object, if sanctioned by a number of share- holders representing three-quarters of the total.

Chapter II. — Capital, Shares, and Rights of the Shareholders.

Art. VI. The capital of the Company is fixed at £20,000, divided into 2000 shares of £10 each — already subscribed and paid, which shares will pay neither interest nor dividend.

Art. VII. Each shareholder will have the right to effect contracts relating to his share with the approval of the Directors, and only according to their stipulations. A faithful copy of any contract will be deposited in the head office of the Company, and will be read immediately after the opening of a general meeting of shareholders, and before beginning to treat of other matters. No share will be transferred in the books of the Company in a manner contrary to the stipulations of such contracts without previous consent of the Directory. No shareholder will be recognised in any general meeting contrary to the stipulations of these contracts.

Art. VIII. The President of the Company for the time of its duration will act as mandatory of all the shareholders residing abroad, excepting those shareholders who give notice in writing that they have named another shareholder to act individually in their name. The shareholders residing abroad will have the right to meet to examine accounts and investigate the business of the Company, and can at this meeting name their mandatories to represent them in Paraguay. They and their representatives will vote unanimously with the shares which they hold.

Art. IX. Each six months a general meeting will be called at the head office of the Company on the first Monday in September, and the first Monday in March, at 3 p.m. Fifteen days beforehand notice will be given, with a list of the matters to be discussed. Any other matter dispatched in such meeting without a previous notice of forty-eight hours will be considered null and void. If a majority of shares are not represented by either the presence of the shareholders or of their representatives no such meeting nor any other meeting will be valid, but will remain adjourned from week to week for twenty-eight days. After the termination of this period, any number of shareholders will constitute a legal meeting.

Art. X. The half-yearly meeting of shareholders will elect Directors and President, and will have full power to investigate matters and examine the business of the Company. The votes at all meetings will be by shares, counting each share as one vote.

Art. XI. An extraordinary meeting can be called at any time by the President, and will be held at the head office of the Company after the shareholders have received notice a week before date of such meeting. Such meeting will have all the rights of the half-yearly meeting, and if representing a twentieth part of the shares can call at any time a general meeting of shareholders, giving to the President, with their signatures at the foot, fifteen days notice.

Art. XII. The first Directory will consist of four persons whose functions will be honorary: William Lane (President), Alfred Walker, Charles Holyer, and James Mooney, who will manage the business of the Company for six months. Three Directors form a quorum. The Directors will be eligible for re-election, in case of a vacancy it must be filled by the President until a general meeting can be called.

Art. XIII. The functions and duties of the Directors are: (a) To manage all the society's interests, and work for their greatest advantage; (b) to fix the Budget and authorise extraordinary matters; (c) dictate internal regulations; (d) authorise contracts made by the Society including those of buying and selling; (e) present at the general meetings the balances and reports, according to Art. XVI.

Art. XIV. The functions and duties of the President are: (a) To represent the Society legally; (b) to convene ordinary and extraordinary meetings according to the statutes and with consent of the Directory; (c) to preside at the meetings and decide the voting in cases of equality of votes in the sessions of the Directory; (d) to execute the resolutions of the meetings and of the Directory, and to provide for the carrying out of these statutes; (e) to sign, together with one Director, the provisions and definite titles of the shares, receipts, transfers, contracts, acts, and other documents that emanate from the Society, and carry them through; (f) to sign, together with one Director, the writings relating to the concession of the land in favour of the Company by the Superior Government.

Art. XV. There must be elected an Auditor every six months at the general meeting.

Art. XVI. The Directors will present to the Auditor a report of the Company every three months, which will be published for three days, and each six months a balance and detailed account of the operations of the Company, with proposals for Reserves, etc. The Auditor will examine and give his report in this respect. Ten days before the general meeting the report and balance sheet will be published in a newspaper which circulates in the vicinity of the Company.

Art.; XVII. A majority of three-fourths of the shares will be required at an extraordinary meeting called to resolve the following: Dissolution of the Company, prolonging its duration, fusion with other companies, reduction of capital, increase of capital, change of object, all other modifications of the Constitution.

APPENDIX C: Revisions of Clauses

After the arrival of the second contingent from Australia certain regulations were altered in order to check the dictatorial powers of the directors, and many new ones were established. After revision, Clauses 10 and 11 read thus :

Executive Authority. 10. Director and a Board of Management elected by a two-thirds majority in a general ballot, to be sole executive authority.
Departmental Authority. 11. Superintendents elected by a two-thirds majority of departmental ballot to be sole departmental authority, subject to the Director, and Board of Management.

The following is the text of the other supplementary clauses introduced after the Socialists had reached New Australia. Note the multiplication of office-holders — directors, deputy-directors, managers, superintendents, agents, etc.

INITIATIVE.
30. Any twenty-five members may at any time take the initiative and convene a public meeting, of which seven days notice shall be given, for the consideration of any stated business; such meeting may select its own chairman, and, provided a two-thirds majority be obtained at a ballot vote seven clear days after such meeting, the decision arrived at shall be held valid and become law.

MEMBERS.
31. Members of the Association shall be those who have (a) satisfied the Board of Management or any

authorised agent as to their desirability; (b) signed the constitution and have complied with all conditions.

MEMBERSHIP LIST.
32. The membership list shall be kept in the central office of the Association in Paraguay, and the persons whose names are on the list shall be regarded as constituting the said Association, and the list shall be subject to alteration by the Director on twenty-one days notice being given of any intended addition or erasure of names.

MANAGEMENT.
33. The control of the Association shall be in the hands of a Director and a Board of Management.

COMPOSITION of board.
34. The Board of Management shall be composed of the Director and a Deputy Director, and two managers from each community, elected by a two thirds majority vote of all voters.

35. The Board of Management may receive any written suggestions, complaints, or other matters which members may wish to bring before it.

36. Re-arrangement of representation upon the Board of Management may be made at any time by a two-thirds majority vote of all voters.

FUNCTIONS OF BOARD.
37. The Board of Management shall have full authority (a) to expend the funds in its hands as may seem to it best for the good of the Association ; (b) to make such terms and arrangements with the Government of Paraguay as may conduce to the maintenance of cordial and loyal relationship with such Government ; (c) it

shall have all other powers necessary for the carrying on of the purposes of the Association.

EXERCISE OF AUTHORITY.
38. The Director shall exercise the authority, and execute the recommendations and resolutions of the Board of Management, excepting only the expending of the general funds of the Association.

DEPUTY DIRECTOR.
39. The Deputy Director shall supervise all departments, and shall give a general monthly report of all work done in each.

SUPERINTENDENTS.
40. Departmental Superintendents shall supervise all work in their particular department ; shall faithfully keep a job time sheet, which they shall supply to the Deputy Director in their respective communities, at least once a week, and shall have full control of, and be responsible for, all tools and materials in their department.

TREASURER.
41. Election: A Treasurer shall be elected by a two-thirds majority vote of all voters.
42. Functions : He shall have charge of the bank books of the Association and shall pay no money except by order of the Board of Management. He shall produce vouchers for all cash payments, and any securities he may hold in hand at every audit of accounts. He shall, on receipt of a written notice, signed by the Director and any three of the Board of Management, deliver up to the Director, within seven days, all books, monies, cheques, and other property of the Association which he may possess.
43. Suspension: He shall be subject to suspension by

the Director pending notification to the members of the Association, who may by a two-thirds majority declare the office vacant, and elect another Treasurer at any time.

SECRETARY.
44. Election : The Secretary shall be elected by a two-thirds majority vote of all voters.
45. Functions: He shall sign all official letters and announcements of the Board of Management. He shall receive all monies for the Board of Management and put them at once into the bank named by the Board, forwarding the deposit slip to the Treasurer within three days of making the deposit. He shall be under the instructions of the Director, and shall perform such duties as may be assigned to him. He shall keep for reference all reports and correspondence received by the Board of Management, and copies of all reports and correspondence emanating from the Board of Management. Any member may examine the records of the Association at any time and may request a copy of any specified record at any time,
46. Suspension : He shall be subject to suspension by the Director pending notification to the members, who may by a two-thirds majority declare the office vacant and elect another Secretary at any time.

EDUCATION.
47. It shall be incumbent on all children, between the ages of 6 and 15 years, to attend the Association schools. Children who will not attend school shall be compelled to work.

CO-OPERATION IN WOMEN'S WORK.
48. It shall be incumbent on all women to organise for assisting in communal work to the best of their ability,

and for this purpose the women in each settlement shall form themselves into a committee for the purpose of deciding upon and apportioning the work to be done by each.

49. In case of non-fulfilment of duties apportioned by such committee they shall have power to report the same to the Board of Management, who will deal with the matter as provided for.

MARRIAGE.

50. The Association may at its discretion prohibit the marriage of any man under 18 years of age or any woman under 16 years of age.

MEMBERSHIP.

51. Qualification: Members of the Association shall be those who have satisfied the Board of Management, or their authorised agents, as to their desirability, and signed the constitution.

52. Disqualification : The following shall not be admitted to membership : (a) Any not knowing English so as to understand and be understood, excepting relatives or sweethearts of members; (b) any person of colour including any married to persons of colour; (c) any living together otherwise than in lawful marriage; (d) any of questionable reputation ; (e) any person of such unsound health as would render him or her a danger or a burden to the community; any objectionable by reason of past disloyalty to the labour movement, or such as are clearly opposed to the common good.

PAYMENTS.

53. Every member, by act of joining the Association, agrees to subscribe to its funds all he may possess when he is finally enrolled, tradesmen's tools and personal effects excepted. Such subscriptions to be not

less than £30 for every male adult above the age of eighteen years.

VOLUNTEERS.
54. Volunteers will be enrolled on the payment of a preliminary fee of £10, which sum remains the property of the Association and cannot be withdrawn.

FREIGHT AND PASSAGE.
55. All charges of freight, passage etc., from the point of departure to the colony, to be defrayed by such volunteers.

PROBATION.
56. At the expiration of three months from the date of their arrival in the colony, all volunteers will be required to complete the necessary conditions of membership, or leave the colony at their own expense.

WIVES AND SINGLE WOMEN.
57. Wives of members are admitted free; also all single women between the ages of 16 and 25 years.

EXCEPTIONS.
58. Exceptions may be made to all of the above at the discretion of the Board of Management ; or its duly authorised agents.

AGENTS.
59. The Board of Management, with the consent of members, shall appoint agents and such other officers as will enable organisation to be effectually conducted, and shall see that such officers are acceptable to, and have the confidence of, all members in their respective localities.
60. To facilitate organisation, groups shall be formed by authorised agents whenever convenient, and shall be

recognised as the centre of the Association in their respective districts.

61. No agent shall bind the Association to the carrying of any contract by a greater bond than the deposit of such sums as may be at the time in his hands, but he may, at his discretion agree by such deposits, to increase the bond at a future date.

62. The authorised agents shall supervise emigration so as to lighten, as far as possible, the attendant hardships; shall see that every member is provided with personal necessaries, and that carriage is available, as. far as possible, for personal effects ; shall advise whenever necessary, and shall make regulations as may seem desirable for the well-being of emigrating members.

ADVANTAGES TO NON-MEMBERS.

63. The Association offers grants of lands to individuals, or groups of individuals, not members of the Association, on terms to be arranged between such individuals and the Board of Management or its duly authorised agents. Such terms to be approved of by a two-thirds majority vote of all voters.

AMENDMENT.

64. Amendment of this constitution and regulations to be made only by a two-thirds majority vote of all voters.

APPENDIX D: 'LABOUR-CHECK' SYSTEM.

1. Each adult member of the Association is entitled to a credit of $4.20 per week; minors between the ages of 15 and 18 $4; children as below.

2. A list of prices of articles likely to be required, will be kept posted in the store. The storekeeper to order any articles asked for, if a credit exists to the amount ordered and the article can be obtained in Asuncion.

3. All articles grown on the settlement must be sold through the store. Prices to be fixed by a committee, consisting of the Director, the Secretary, and the Storekeeper, and as far as possible at current rates.

4. Members who receive their food from the cooperative mess will form a committee, and instruct the cooks at what rate they can draw from each credit.

5 If the quantity of any article be limited, and the demand greater than the supply, the said article shall be divided among the applicants.

6. Each person over 15 years of age is also entitled to a clothing allowance of $2 per week; under 15 years, $1 per week. The accumulation under this rule to be solely spent on necessary articles of clothing, ordered through the store.

7. A receiving book shall be kept by the Storekeeper at each settlement, and all articles, whether produced or imported, be entered therein, and copies furnished to the central office.

8. The scale of diet, both as to quantities and prices, shall be adjustable from time to time.

9. The Board of Management is empowered to reduce any person's credit for proved offences.

May 21st, 1895. NOTE.— The Paraguayan dollar was worth, in 1806 roughly sixpence of English money.

APPENDIX E: THE IDEAL HOME.

In January I 1901, when Cosme Colony had been in existence six and a half years, the citizens were still living in such squalid dens that the community drew up an official standard of design for dwellings, to be erected 'one for all and all for one,' the following was the standard (by no means realised) adopted for size and build of Cosme dwelling-houses:

Class 1. For Single Men or Women:
A single-roomed cottage with floor space to the amount of 144 sq. ft. with walls eight feet high (from floor to the top of wall plate), of sawn slabs with smooth side outward and pugged within; one fireplace and chimney; two windows (maximum size, 3 by 2 ft,) and one door, or two doors and one window; verandah 5 ft. wide on one side of cottage; earthen floor; posts of round hardwood; plates, rafters, and battens sawn; gable ends of sawn boards; roof of whatever material may be most convenient — thatch or shingle.

Class 2. For Families with not more than Two Children, the elder of whom is not more than five years old:
A two-roomed cottage with floor space to the amount of 288 sq. ft.; walls 8 ft. high, pugged on both sides; partition 8 ft. high, of boards; fireplace and chimney to living room. Floor and general manner of building as for cottage Class 1 Front verandah 5 ft. wide, back verandah 7 ft. wide. Detached kitchen with floor space of 120 sq. ft. in addition to fireplace. Fireplace fitted with oven; walls of kitchen 6J ft. high with projecting eaves.

Class 3. For Larger or Older Families than Class 2:

For each child or pair of children, more than two children, under four years of age, an additional room will be provided by making verandah rooms of the back verandah, the walls of which rooms will be of sawn timber. In families where there are children of each sex over six years of age, arrangements to be made for separate bedroom accommodation.

APPENDIX F: Preface to Freeland: A Social Anticipation

The economic and social order of the modern world exhibits a strange enigma, which only a prosperous thoughtlessness can regard with indifference or, indeed, without a shudder. We have made such splendid advances in art and science that the unlimited forces of nature have been brought into subjection, and only await our command to perform for us all our disagreeable and onerous tasks, and to wring from the soil and prepare for use whatever man, the master of the world, may need. As a consequence, a moderate amount of labour ought to produce inexhaustible abundance for everyone born of woman; and yet all these glorious achievements have not--as Stuart Mill forcibly says--been able to mitigate one human woe. And, what is more, the ever-increasing facility of producing an abundance has proved a curse to multitudes who lack necessaries because there exists no demand for the many good and useful things which they are able to produce. The industrial activity of the present day is a ceaseless confused struggle with the various symptoms of the dreadful evil known as 'over-production.' Protective duties, cartels and trusts, guild agitations, strikes--all these are but the desperate resistance offered by the classes engaged in production to the inexorable consequences of the apparently so absurd, but none the less real, phenomenon that increasing facility in the production of wealth brings ruin and misery in its train.

That science stands helpless and perplexed before this enigma, that no beam of light has yet penetrated and dispelled the gloom of this--the social--problem, though that problem has exercised the minds of the noblest and best of to-day, is in part due to the fact that the solution has been sought in a wrong direction.

Let us see, for example, what Stuart Mill says upon this subject: 'I looked forward ... to a future' ... whose views (and institutions) ... shall be 'so firmly grounded in reason and in the true exigencies of life that they shall not, like all former and present creeds, religious, ethical, and political, require to be periodically thrown off and replaced by others.'

Yet more plainly does Laveleye express himself in the same sense at the close of his book 'De la Propriété': 'There is an order of human affairs *which is the best ... God knows it and wills it*. Man must discover and introduce it.'

It is therefore an *absolutely best, eternal order* which both are waiting for; although, when we look more closely, we find that both ought to know they are striving after the impossible. For Mill, a few lines before the above remarkable passage, points out that all human things are in a state of constant flux; and upon this he bases his conviction that existing institutions can be only transitory. Therefore, upon calm reflection, he would be compelled to admit that the same would hold in the future, and that consequently unchangeable human institutions will never exist. And just so must we suppose that Laveleye, with his '*God knows it and wills it*,' would have to admit that it could *not* be man's task either to discover or to introduce the absolutely best order known only to God. He is quite correct in saying that if there be really an absolutely best order, God alone knows it; but since it cannot be the office of science to wait upon Divine revelation, and since such an absolutely best order could be introduced by God alone and not by men, and therefore the revelation of the Divine will would not help us in the least, so it must logically follow, from the admission that the knowing and the willing of the absolutely good appertain to God, that man has not to strive after this absolutely good, but after the *relatively best*, which alone is intelligible to and attainable by him.

And thus it is in fact. The solution of the social problem is not to be sought in the discovery of an *absolutely good* order of society, but in that of the *relatively best*--that is, of such an order of human institutions as best corresponds to the contemporary conditions of human existence. The existing arrangements of society call for improvement, not because they are out of harmony with our longing for an absolutely good state of things, but because it can be shown to be possible to replace them by others more in accordance with the contemporary conditions of human existence. Darwin's law of evolution in nature teaches us that when the actual social arrangements have ceased to be the relatively best--that is, those which best correspond to the contemporary conditions of human existence--their abandonment is not only possible but simply inevitable. For in the struggle for existence that which is out of date not only *may* but *must* give place to that which is more in harmony with the actual conditions. And this law also teaches us that all the characters of any organic being whatever are the results of that being's struggle for existence in the conditions in which it finds itself. If, now, we bring together these various hints offered us by the doctrine of evolution, we see the following to be the only path along which the investigation of the social problem can be pursued so as to reach the goal:

First, we must inquire and establish under what particular conditions of existence the actual social arrangements were evolved.

Next we must find out whether these same conditions of existence still subsist, or whether others have taken their place.

If others have taken their place, it must be clearly shown whether the new conditions of existence are compatible with the old arrangements; and, if not, what alterations of the latter are required.

The new arrangements thus discovered must and will contain that which we are justified in looking for as the 'solution of the social problem.'

When I applied this strictly scientific method of investigation to the social problem, I arrived four years ago at the following conclusions, to the exposition of which I devoted my book on 'The Laws of Social Evolution,' published at that time:

The actual social arrangements are the necessary result of the human struggle for existence when the productiveness of labour was such that a single worker could produce, by the labour of his own hands, more than was indispensable to the sustenance of his animal nature, but not enough to enable him to satisfy his higher needs. With only this moderate degree of productiveness of labour, the exploitage of man by man was the only way by which it was possible to ensure to *individuals* wealth and leisure, those fundamental essentials to higher culture. But as soon as the productiveness of labour reaches the point at which it is sufficient to satisfy also the highest requirements of every worker, the exploitage of man by man not only ceases to be a necessity of civilisation, but becomes an obstacle to further progress by hindering men from making full use of the industrial capacity to which they have attained.

For, as under the domination of exploitage the masses have no right to more of what they produce than is necessary for their bare subsistence, demand is cramped by limitations which are quite independent of the possible amount of production. Things for which there is no demand are valueless, and therefore will not be produced; consequently, under the exploiting system, society does not produce that amount of wealth which the progress of science and technical art has made possible, but only that infinitely smaller amount which suffices for the bare subsistence of the masses and the luxury of the few. Society wishes to employ the whole of the surplus of the productive power in the creation of instruments of labour--that is, it wishes to convert it into capital; but this is impossible, since the quantity of utilisable capital is strictly dependent upon the quantity of commodities to be produced by the aid of this capital. The utilisation of all the proceeds of such highly productive labour is therefore dependent upon the creation of a new social order which shall guarantee to every worker the enjoyment of the full proceeds of his own work. And since impartial investigation further shows that this new order is not merely indispensable to further progress in civilisation, but is also thoroughly in harmony with the natural and acquired characteristics of human society, and consequently is met by no inherent and permanent obstacle, it is evident that in the natural process of human evolution this new order must necessarily come into being.

When I placed this conclusion before the public four years ago, I assumed, as something self-evident, that I was announcing a doctrine which was not by any means an isolated novelty; and I distinctly said so in the preface to the 'Laws of Social Evolution.' I fully understood that there must be some connecting bridge between the so-called classical economics and the newly discovered truths; and I was convinced that in a not distant future either others or myself would discover this bridge. But in expounding the consequences springing from the above-mentioned general principles, I at first allowed an error to escape my notice. That ground-rent and undertaker's profit--that is, the payment which the landowner demands for the use of his land, and the claim of the so-called work-giver to the produce of the worker's labour--are incompatible with the claim of the worker to the produce of his own labour, and that consequently in the course of social evolution ground-rent and undertaker's profit must become obsolete and must be given up--this I perceived; but with respect to the interest of capital I adhered to the classical-orthodox view that this was a postulate of progress which would survive all the phases of evolution.

As palliation of my error I may mention that it was the opponents of capital themselves--and Marx in particular--who confirmed me in it, or, more correctly, who prevented me from distinctly perceiving the basis upon which interest essentially rests. To tear oneself away from long-cherished views is in itself extremely difficult; and when, moreover, the men who attack the old views base their attack point after point upon error, it becomes only too easy to mistake the weakness of the attack for impregnability in the thing attacked. Thus it happened with me. Because I saw that what had been hitherto advanced against capital and interest was altogether untenable, I felt myself absolved from the task of again and independently inquiring whether there were no better, no really valid, arguments against the absolute and permanent necessity of interest. Thus, though interest is, in reality, as little compatible with associated labour carried on upon the principle of perfect economic justice as are ground-rent and the undertaker's profit, I was prevented by this fundamental error from arriving at satisfactory views concerning the constitution and character of the future forms of organisation based upon the principle of free organisation. *That* and *wherefore* economic freedom and justice must eventually be practically realised, I had shown; on the other hand, *how* this phase of evolution was to be brought about I was not able to make fully clear. Yet I did not ascribe this inability to any error of mine in thinking the subject out, but believed it to reside in the nature of the subject itself. I reasoned that institutions the practical shaping of which belongs to the future could not be known in detail before they were evolved. Just as those former generations, which knew nothing of the modern joint-stock company, could not possibly form an exact and perfect idea of the nature and working of this institution even if they had conceived the principle upon which it is based, so I held it to be impossible to-day to possess a clear and connected idea of those future economic forms which cannot be evolved until the principle of the free association of labour has found its practical realisation.

I was slow in discovering the above-mentioned connection of my doctrine of social evolution with the orthodox system of economy. The most clear-sighted minds of three centuries have been at work upon that system; and if a new doctrine is to win acceptance, it is absolutely necessary that its propounder should not merely refute the old doctrine and expose its errors, but should trace back and lay open to its remotest source the particular process of thought which led these heroes of our science into their errors. It is not enough to show *that* and *wherefore* their theses were false; it must also be made clear *how* and *wherefore* those thinkers arrived at their false theses, what it was that forced them--despite all their sagacity--to hold such theses as correct though they are simply absurd when viewed in the light of truth. I pondered in vain over this enigma, until suddenly, like a ray of sunlight, there shot into the darkness of my doubt the discovery that in its essence my work was nothing but the necessary outcome of what others had achieved--that my theory was in no way out of harmony with the numerous theories of my predecessors, but that rather, when thoroughly understood, it was the very truth after which all the other economists had been searching, and upon the track of which--and this I held to be decisive--I had been thrown, not by my own sagacity, but solely by the mental labours of my great predecessors. In other words, *the solution of the social problem offered by me is the very solution of the economic problem which the science of political economy has been incessantly seeking from its first rise down to the present day.*

But, I hear it asked, does political economy possess such a problem--one whose solution it has merely attempted but not arrived at? For it is remarkable that in our science the widest diversity of opinions co-exists with the most dogmatic orthodoxy. Very few draw from the existence of the numberless antagonistic opinions the self-evident conclusion that those opinions are erroneous, or at least unproved; and none are willing to admit that--like their opponents--they are merely seeking the truth, and are not in possession of it. So prevalent is this tenacity of opinion which puts faith in the place of knowledge that the fact that every science owes its origin to a problem is altogether forgotten. This problem may afterwards find its solution, and therewith the science will have achieved its purpose; but without a problem there is no investigation--consequently, though there may be knowledge, there will be no science. Clear and simple cognisances do not stimulate the human mind to that painstaking, comprehensive effort which is the necessary antecedent of science; in brief, a science can arise only when things are under consideration which are not intelligible directly and without profound reflection--things, therefore, which contain a problem.

Thus, political economy must have had its problem, its enigma, out of the attempts to solve which it had its rise. This problem is nothing else but the question '*Why do we not become richer in proportion to our increasing capacity of producing wealth?*' To this question a satisfactory answer can no more be given to-day than could be given three centuries ago--at the time, that is, when the problem first arose in view, not of a previously existing phenomenon to which the human mind had then had its attention drawn for the first time, but of a phenomenon which was then making its first appearance.

With unimportant and transient exceptions (which, it may be incidentally remarked, are easily explicable from what follows) antiquity and the Middle Ages had no political economy. This was not because the men of those times were not sharp-sighted enough to discover the sources of wealth, but because to them there was nothing enigmatical about those sources of wealth. The nations became richer the more progress they made in the art of producing; and this was so self-evident and clear that, very rightly, no one thought it necessary to waste words about it. It was not until the end of the sixteenth and the beginning of the seventeenth centuries of our era, therefore scarcely three hundred years ago, that political economy as a distinct science arose.

It is impossible for the unprejudiced eye to escape seeing what the first political economists sought for--what the problem was with which they busied themselves. They stood face to face with the enigmatical fact that increasing capacity of production is not necessarily accompanied or followed by an increase of wealth; and they sought to explain this fact. Why this remarkable fact then first made its appearance will be clearly seen from what follows; it is unquestionable *that* it then appeared, for the whole system of these first political economists, the so-called Mercantilists, had no other aim than to demonstrate that the increase of wealth depends not, as everybody had until then very naturally believed, upon increasing productiveness of labour, but upon something else, that something else being, in the opinion of the Mercantilists, money. Notwithstanding what may be called the tangible absurdity of this doctrine, it remained unquestioned for generations; nay, to be candid, most men still cling to it--a fact which would be inconceivable did not the doctrine offer a very simple and plausible explanation of the enigmatical phenomenon that increasing capacity of production does not necessarily bring with it a corresponding increase of wealth.

But it is equally impossible for the inquiring human mind to remain permanently blind to the fact that money and wealth are two very different things, and that therefore some other solution must be looked for of the problem, the existence of which is not to be denied. The Physiocrats found this second explanation in the assertion that the soil was the source and origin of all wealth, whilst human labour, however highly developed it might be, could add nothing to what was drawn from the soil, because labour itself consumed what it produced. This may look like the first application of the subsequently discovered natural law of the conservation of force; and--notwithstanding its obvious absurdity--it was seriously believed in because it professed to explain what seemed otherwise inexplicable. Between the labourer's means of subsistence, the amount of labour employed, and the product, there is by no means that quantitative relation which is to be found in the conversion of one physical force into another. Human labour produces more or less in proportion as it is better or worse applied; for production does not consist in converting labour into things that have a value, but in using labour to produce such things out of natural objects. A child can understand this, yet the acutest thinkers of the eighteenth century denied it with the approval of the best of their contemporaries and of not the worst of their epigones, because they could not otherwise explain the strange problem of human economics.

Then arose that giant of our science, one of the greatest minds of which humanity can boast--Adam Smith. He restored the ancient wisdom of our ancestors, and also clearly and irrefutably demonstrated what they had only instinctively recognised--namely, that the increase of wealth depends upon the productiveness of human labour. But while he threw round this truth the enduring ramparts of his logic and of his sound understanding, he altogether failed to see that the actual facts directly contradicted his doctrine. He saw that wealth did *not* increase step by step with the increased productiveness of labour; but he believed he had discovered the cause of this in the mercantilistic and physiocratic sins of the past. In his day the historical sense was not sufficiently developed to save him from the error of confounding the--erroneous--explanations of an existing evil with its causes. Hence he believed that the course of economic events would necessarily correspond fully with the restored laws of a sound understanding--that is, that wealth would necessarily increase step by step with the capacity of producing it, if only production were freed from the legislative restraints and fiscal fetters which cramped it.

But even this delusion could not long prevail. Ricardo was the first of the moderns who perceived that wealth did not increase in proportion to industrial capacity, even when production and trade were, as Smith demanded, freed from State interference and injury. He hit upon the expedient of finding the cause of this incongruity in the nature of labour itself. Since labour is the only source of value, he said, it cannot increase value. A thing is worth as much as the quantity of labour put into it;

consequently, when with increasing productiveness of labour the amount of labour necessary to the production of a thing is diminished, then the value of that thing diminishes also. Hence no increase in the productiveness of labour can increase the total sum of values. This, however, is a fundamental mistake, for what depends upon the amount of labour is merely the *relative* value of things--the exchange relation in which they stand to other things. This is so self-evident that Ricardo himself cannot avoid expressly stating that he is speaking of merely the 'relative' value of things; nevertheless, this relative value-- which, strictly speaking, is nothing but a value relation, the relation of values--is treated by him as if it were absolute value.

And yet Ricardo's error is a not less important step in the evolution of doctrine than those of his previously mentioned predecessors. It signifies the revival of the original problem of political economy, which had been lost sight of since Adam Smith; and Ricardo's follower, Marx, is in a certain sense right when, with bitter scorn, he denounces as 'vulgar economists' those who, persistently clinging to Smith's optimism, see in the *productiveness* of labour the measure of the increase of *actual* wealth. For all that was brought against Ricardo by his opponents was known by him as well as or better than by them; only he knew what had escaped their notice, or what they saw no obligation to take note of in their theory--namely, that the actual facts directly contradicted the doctrine. It by no means escaped Ricardo that his attempted reconciliation of the theory with the great problem of economics was absurd; and Marx has most clearly shown the absurdity of it. The latter speaks of the alleged dependence of value, not upon the productiveness of labour, but upon the effort put forth by the labourer, as the 'fetishism' of industry; this relation, being unnatural, contrary to the nature of things, ought therefore--and this, again, is Marx's contribution to the progress of the science--to be referred back to an unnatural ultimate cause residing, not in the nature of things, but in human arrangements. And in looking for this ultimate cause, he, like his great predecessors, comes extremely near to the truth, but, after all, glides past without seeing it.

On this road, which leads to truth past so many errors, the last stage is the hypothesis set up by the so-called Historical School of political economy--the hypothesis, namely, that there exists in the nature of things a gulf between economic theory and practice, which makes it quite conceivable that the principles that are correct *in thesi* do not coincide with the real course of industrial life. The existence of the problem is thereby more fully established than ever, but its solution is placed outside of the domain of theoretical cognisance. For the Historical School is perfectly correct in maintaining that the abstractions of the current economic doctrine are practically useless, and that this is true not only of some of them, but of all. The real human economy does *not* obey those laws which the theorists have abstractedly deduced from economic phenomena. Hence it is only possible either that the human economy is by its very nature unfitted to become the object of scientific abstraction and cognisance, or that the abstractions hitherto made have been erroneous--erroneous, that is, not in the sense of being actually out of harmony with phenomena from which they are correctly and logically deduced, but in the sense of being theoretically erroneous, deduced according to wrong principles, and therefore useless both *in abstracto* and *in concreto*.

Of these alternatives only the second can, in reality, be correct. There is absolutely no reasonable ground for supposing that the laws which regulate the economic activity of men should be beyond human cognisance; and still less ground is there for assuming that such laws do not exist at all. We must therefore suppose that the science which seeks to discover these laws has hitherto failed to attain its object simply because it has been upon the wrong road--that is, that the principles of political economy are erroneous because, in deducing them from the economic phenomena, some fact has been overlooked, some mistake in reasoning has been committed. There *must* be a correct solution of the problem of political economy; and the solution of the social problem derived from the theory of social evolution offers at once the key to the other.

The correct answer to the question, 'Why are we not richer in proportion to the increase in our productive capacity?' is this: *Because wealth does not consist in what can be produced, but in what is actually produced; the actual production, however, depends not merely upon the amount of productive power, but also upon the extent of what is required, not merely upon the possible supply, but also upon the possible demand: the current social arrangements, however, prevent the demand from increasing to the same extent as the productive capacity.* In other words: We do not produce that wealth which our present capacity makes it possible for us to produce, but only so much as we have use for; and this use depends, not upon our capacity of producing, but upon our capacity of consuming.

It is now plain why the economic problem of the disparity between the possible and the actual increase of wealth is of so comparatively recent a date. Antiquity and the middle ages knew nothing of this problem, because human labour was not then productive enough to do more than provide and maintain the means of production after covering the consumption of the masses and the possessors of property. There was in those ages a demand for all the things which labour was then able to produce; full employment could be made of any increase of capacity to create wealth; no one could for a moment be in doubt as to the purpose which the increased power of producing had served; there was no economic problem to call into existence a special science of political economy. Then came the Renaissance; the human mind awoke out of its thousand years of hibernation; the great inventions and discoveries rapidly followed one upon another; division of labour and the mobilisation of capital gave a powerful impulse to production; and now, for the first time, the productiveness of labour became so great, and the impossibility of using as much as labour could produce became so evident, that men were compelled to face the perplexing fact which finds expression in the economic problem.

That three centuries should have had to elapse before the solution could be found, is in perfect harmony with the other fact that it was reserved for these last generations to give us complete control over the forces of nature, and to render it possible for us to *make use* of the knowledge we have acquired. For so long as human production was in the main dependent upon the capacity and strength of human muscles, aided by the muscles of a few domestic animals, more might certainly be produced than would be consumed by the luxury of a few after the bare subsistence of the masses had been provided for; but to afford to *all* men an abundance without excessive labour needed the results of the substitution of the inexhaustible forces of nature for muscular energy. Until this substitution had become possible, it would have availed mankind little to have attained to a knowledge of the ultimate ground of the hindrance to the full utilisation of the then existing powers of production.

For in order that the exploitage of man by man might be put an end to, it was necessary that the amount of producible wealth should not merely exceed the consumption of the few wealthy persons, but should be sufficient to satisfy the higher human needs of all. Economic equity, if it is not to bring about a stagnation in civilisation, assumes that the man who has to depend upon the earnings of his own labour is in a position to enjoy a considerable amount of wealth at the cost of moderate effort. This has become possible only during the last few generations; and herein is to be sought the reason why the great economists of the seventeenth and eighteenth centuries were not able to rise to an unprejudiced critical examination of the true nature and the necessary consequences of the exploiting system of industry. *They* were compelled to regard exploitage as a cruel but eternally unavoidable condition of the progress of civilisation; for when they lived it was and it always had been a necessity of civilisation, and they could not justly be expected to anticipate such a fundamental revolution in the conditions of human existence as must necessarily precede the passage from exploitage to economic equity.

So long as the exploitage of man by man was considered a necessary and eternal institution, there existed no motive to prompt men to subject it to a closer critical investigation; and in the absence of such an investigation its influence upon the nature and extent of demand could not be discovered. The old economists were therefore *compelled* to believe it chimerical to think of demand as falling short of production; for they said, quite correctly, that man produces only to consume. Here, with them, the question of demand was done with, and every possibility of the discovery of the true connection cut off. Their successors, on the other hand, who have all been witnesses of the undreamt-of increase of the productiveness of labour, have hitherto been prevented, by their otherwise well-justified respect for the authority of the founders of our science, from adequately estimating the economic importance of this revolution in the conditions of labour. The classical system of economics is based upon a conception of the world which takes in all the affairs of life, is self-consistent, and is supported by all the past teachings of the great forms of civilisation; and if we would estimate the enormous force with which this doctrine holds us bound, we must remember that even those who were the first to recognise its incongruity with existing facts were unable to free themselves from its power. They persisted in believing in it, though they perceived its incompatibility with the facts, and knew therefore that it was false.

This glance at the historical evolution of economic doctrine opens the way to the rectification of all the errors of which the different schools of political economy have--even in their quest after truth--been guilty. It is seen that the great inquirers and thinkers of past centuries, in their vast work of investigation and analysis of economic facts, approached so very near to the full and complete cognisance of the true connection of all phenomena, that it needed but a little more labour in order to construct a thoroughly harmonious definitive economic theory based upon the solution, at last discovered, of the long vexed problem.

I zealously threw myself into this task, and had proceeded with it a considerable way--to the close of a thick first volume, containing a new treatment of the theory of value; but when at work on the classical theory of capital, I made a discovery which at once threw a ray of light into the obscurity that had until then made the practical realisation of the forms of social organisation impossible. *I perceived that capitalism stops the growth of wealth, not--as Marx has it--by stimulating 'production for the market,' but by preventing the consumption of the surplus produce; and that interest, though not unjust, will nevertheless in a condition of economic justice become superfluous and objectless.* These two fundamental truths will be found treated in detail in chapters xxiv. and xviii.; but I cannot refrain here from doing justice to the manes of Marx, by acknowledging unreservedly his service in having been the first to proclaim--though he misunderstood it and argued illogically-- the connection between the problem of value and modern capitalism.

I consider the theoretical and practical importance of these new truths to be incalculable. Not merely do they at once give to the theory of social evolution the unity and harmony of a definitive whole, but, what is more, they show the way to an immediate practical realisation of the principles formulated by this theory. If it is possible for the community to provide the capital for production with out thereby doing injury to either the principle of perfect individual freedom or to that of justice, *if interest can be dispensed with without introducing communistic control in its stead, then there no longer stands any positive obstacle in the way of the establishment of the free social order.*

My intense delight at making this discovery robbed me of the calm necessary to the prosecution of the abstract investigations upon which I was engaged. Before my mind's eye arose scenes which the reader will find in the following pages--tangible, living pictures of a commonwealth based upon the most perfect freedom and equity, and which needs nothing to convert it into a reality but the will of a number of resolute men. It happened to me as it may have happened to Bacon of Verulam when his studies for the 'Novum Organon' were interrupted by the vision of his 'Nova Atlantis'--with this difference, however, that his prophetic glance saw the land of social freedom and justice when centuries of bondage still separated him from it, whilst I see it when mankind is already actually equipped ready to step over its threshold. Like him, I felt an irresistible impulse vividly to depict what agitated my mind. Thus, putting aside for awhile the abstract and systematic treatise which I had begun, I wrote this book, which can justly be called 'a political romance,' though it differs from all its predecessors of that category in introducing no unknown and mysterious human powers and characteristics, but throughout keeps to the firm ground of the soberest reality. The scene of the occurrences described by me is no imaginary fairy-land, but a part of our planet well-known to modern geography, which I describe exactly as its discoverers and explorers have done. The men who appear in my narrative are endowed with no supernatural properties and virtues, but are spirit of our spirit, flesh of our flesh; and the motive prompting their economic activity is neither public spirit nor universal philanthropy, but an ordinary and commonplace self-interest. Everything in my 'Freeland' is severely real, only one fiction underlies the whole narrative, namely, that a sufficient number of men possessing a modicum of capacity and strength have actually been found ready to take the step that shall deliver them from the bondage of the exploiting system of economics, and conduct them into the enjoyment of a system of social equity and freedom. Let this one assumption be but realised--and that it will be, sooner or later, I have no doubt, though perhaps not exactly as I have represented--then will 'Freeland' have become a reality, and the deliverance of mankind will have been accomplished. For the age of bondage is past; that control over the forces of nature which the founder of modern natural science, in his 'Nova Atlantis,' predicted as the end of human misery has now been actually acquired. We are prevented from enjoying the fruits of this acquisition, from making full use of the discoveries and inventions of the great intellects of our race, by nothing but the phlegmatic faculty of persistence in old habits which still keeps laws and institutions in force when the conditions that gave rise to them have long since disappeared.

As this book professes to offer, in narrative form, a picture of the actual social life of the future, it follows as a matter of course that it will be exposed, in all its essential features, to the severest professional criticism. To this criticism I submit it, with this observation, that, if my work is to be regarded as a failure, or as the offspring of frivolous fancy, it must be demonstrated that men gifted with a normal average understanding would in any material point arrive at results other than those described by me if they were organised according to the principles which I have expounded; or that those principles contain anything which a sound understanding would not accept as a self-evident postulate of justice as well as of an enlightened self-interest.

I do not imagine that the establishment of the future social order must necessarily be effected exactly in the way described in the following pages. But I certainly think that this would be the best and the simplest way, because it would most speedily and easily lead to the desired result. If economic freedom and justice are to obtain in human society, they must be seriously *determined upon*; and it seems easier to unite a few thousands in such a determination than numberless millions, most of whom are not accustomed to accept the new--let it be ever so clear and self-evident--until it has been embodied in fact.

Nor would I be understood to mean that, supposing there could be found a sufficient number of resolute men to carry out the work of social emancipation, Equatorial Africa must be chosen as the scene of the undertaking. I was led, by reasons stated in the book, to fix upon the remarkable hill country of Central Africa; but similar results could be achieved in many other parts of our planet. I must ask the reader to believe that, in making choice of the scene, I was not influenced by a desire to give the reins to my fancy; on the contrary, the descriptions of the little-known mountains and lakes of Central Africa adhere in all points to sober reality. Any one who doubts this may compare my narrative with the accounts given by Speke, Grant, Livingstone, Baker, Stanley, Emin Pacha, Thomson, Johnston, Fischer--in short, by all who have visited these paradisiacal regions.

Just a few words in conclusion, in justification of the romantic accessories introduced into the exposition of so serious a subject. I might appeal to the example of my illustrious predecessors, of whom I have already mentioned Bacon, the clearest, the acutest, the soberest thinker of all times. But I feel bound to confess that I had a double purpose. In the first place, I hoped by means of vivid and striking pictures to make the difficult questions which form the essential theme of the book acceptable to a wider circle of readers than I could have expected to reach by a dry systematic treatment. In the second place, I wished, by means of the concrete form thus given to a part of my abstractions, to refute by anticipation the criticism that those abstractions, though correct *in thesi*, were nevertheless inapplicable *in praxi*. Whether I have succeeded in these two objects remains to be proved.

THEODOR HERTZKA.

VIENNA: *October* 1889.

[i] Freeland: A Social Anticipation is available at
http://www.gutenberg.org/files/9866/9866-h/9866-h.htm

[ii] The reason the people of Freeland can live in such luxury is that they have a range of 'machinery' at their disposal. Such machinery that, we'll see, the people of New Australia will never come close to producing. Here is the passage in question from 'Freeland: A Social Anticipation': *"Under the name of machinery we here include everything which on the one hand is not a free gift of nature, but the outcome of human effort, and on the other hand is intended to increase the productiveness of human labour. This power has grown to colossal dimensions in Freeland. Our system of railways--the lines above-named are only the four largest, which serve for communication with other countries--has reached a total length of road of about 358,000 miles, of which less than 112,000 miles are main lines, while about 248,000 miles are lines for agricultural and industrial purposes. Our canal system serves mainly for purposes of irrigation and draining, and the total length of its numberless thousands of larger and smaller branches is beyond all calculation, but these canals are navigable for a length of 86,000 miles. Besides the passenger ships already mentioned, there are afloat upon the seas of the world nearly 3,000 of our freight steamers with a total registered tonnage of 14,500,000. On the lakes and rivers of Africa we possess 17,800 larger and smaller steamers with a total register of 5,200,000 tons. The motive power which drives these means of communication and the numberless machines of our agriculture and our factories, our public and private institutions, reaches a total of not less than 245,000,000 horse-power--that is, fully twice the mechanical force employed by the whole of the rest of the world. In Freeland there is brought into use a mechanical force of nearly nine and a-half horse-power per head of the population; and as every registered horse-power is equal to the mechanical force of twelve or thirteen men, the result in labour is the same as if every Freelander without exception*

had about 120 slaves at his disposal. What wonder that we can live like masters, notwithstanding that servitude is not known in Freeland!"

[iii] Voltaire: "The establishment in Paraguay by the Spanish Jesuits appears alone, in some way, the triumph of humanity. It seems to expiate the cruelties of the first conquerors. The Quakers in North America and the Jesuits in South America gave a new spectacle to the world."

[iv] From H.G. Wells 'Socialism and the Family' available here: http://gutenberg.net.au/ebooks13/1303581h.html

[v] 'Ethics of Socialism' http://www.amazon.co.uk/The-Ethics-Socialism-Ernest-Belfort/dp/0543932052

www.ingramcontent.com/pod-product-compliance
Lightning Source LLC
Chambersburg PA
CBHW072212170626
46813CB00003B/903